Scene/Unseen: London's West End Theatres

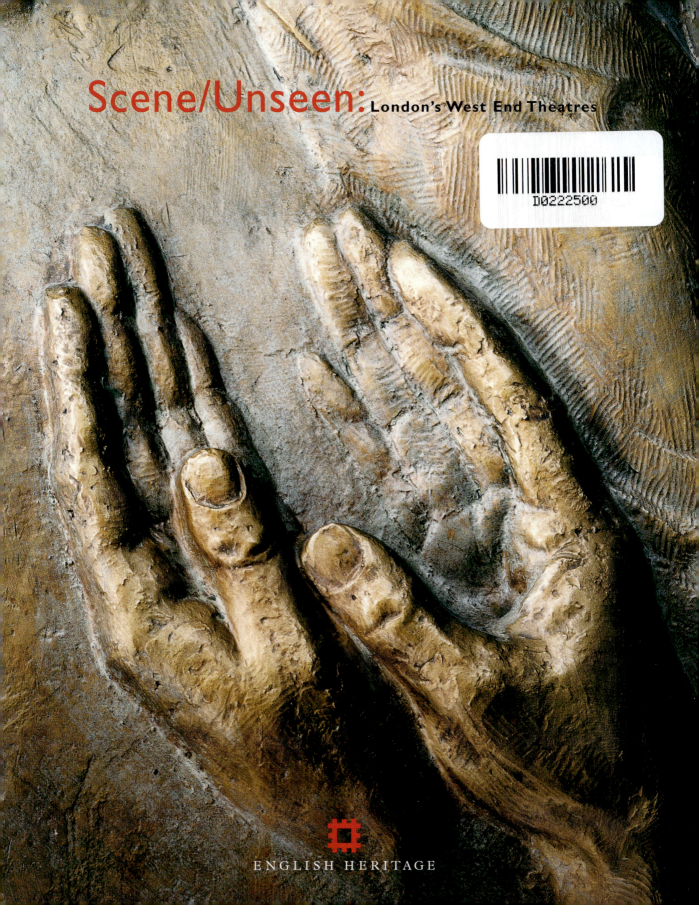

ENGLISH HERITAGE

Scene/Unseen: London's West End Theatres

Photographs by Derek Kendall
with text by Susie Barson, Peter Longman and Joanna Smith
Preface by Fiona Shaw

Published by English Heritage, Kemble Drive, Swindon SN2 2GZ

First published 2003

ISBN 1 873592 74 4

Product code 50751

British Library Cataloguing in Publications Data
A CIP catalogue record for this book is available from the British Library.

Brought to publication by Andrew McLaren and René Rodgers, English Heritage Publishing
Edited by Susan Whimster
Designed by Michael McMann
Printed by Hawthornes

Contents

Acknowledgements 6

Preface by Fiona Shaw 7

Introduction by Susie Barson 8

Front to Back: the anatomy of the West End theatre by Joanna Smith 12

The Photographic Exploration Photographs by Derek Kendall 24

   Front of House 26
      From the outside 27
      The way in 29
      Circulation 33
      Bars 36
      Private spaces 39
      Threshold 41

   The Auditorium 44
      The experience of the auditorium 45
      Seating and sightlines 50
      Theatre boxes 53
      Towards the stage 55
      Hidden from view 57

   Backstage 58
      Around the stage: lighting, traps and props 59
      Scenes and sets 64
      Understage 67
      Above stage: flying systems 72
      Dressing rooms 81
      Costumes 83
      Stage door 86

Living with the Legacy by Peter Longman 88

A Balancing Act: conservation, English Heritage and the West End theatres by Susie Barson 94

West End Theatres: a gazetteer 99

Further Reading 103

Information Sources 104

Acknowledgements

The authors would like to thank all the theatre owners, managers, technicians and front-of-house staff too numerous to mention individually, who allowed us access, took us around the theatres and gave us the benefit of their expertise. The assistance of Heidi Heilbrunn and Mary Galer with the photography was greatly appreciated.

We should also like to thank members of the Archaeology Committee of the Association of British Theatre Technicians for their invaluable advice on the survival and purpose of backstage machinery. The help and support of Rupert Rhymes, who was at the Society of London Theatre when the project started, is also gratefully acknowledged. Current and former trustees and staff of The Theatres Trust – Elspeth Cox, Catherine Croft, Graeme Cruickshank, John Earl, Peter Longman and Fiona Shaw – have given freely of their time and specialised knowledge during the survey and in the preparation of the book. Anne Riches has been especially encouraging and supportive from the outset. Jim Fowler and Beverley Hart at the Theatre Museum were both extremely helpful at the research stage.

From within English Heritage, we have had help and advice from Tony Calladine, Martin Cherry, Andy Donald, John Greenacombe, Tim Jones, David Robinson, Paul Velluet and Humphrey Welfare. June Warrington provided particularly invaluable assistance and Peter Guillery, the project supervisor, gave editorial and other suggestions that were inestimable. We should like to thank all these people.

Preface

by Fiona Shaw

I am one of the lucky ones. As a performer I have toured the world, and not just playing in theatre buildings. I have played in the life-drawing room of Les Beaux Halles in Paris with carved nudes for a proscenium! In New York I've performed in a disused porno theatre on 42nd Street with a rat in the aisle swelling the audience numbers. In Dublin's Phoenix Park I played in a disused munitions factory on the top of a hill, the audience arriving in buses through the deserted village of former army homes. And in London's East End, where I performed T S Eliot's *The Waste Land*, I sat in the almost condemned tenement room in Wilton's Music Hall and looked out at the playground of the school opposite, watching children in their Gap jeans and yashmaks, and thought how like a ghost I must seem if they looked up at the window of a building that had been asleep for over 100 years.

All these experiments came from a need to find a new kind of theatre, for disorientating an audience heightens their faculties of observation even before the piece of theatre begins, as they become alert in unusual surroundings. But I've played my share of traditional theatres too, touring with the Royal Shakespeare Company and the Royal National Theatre. Performing a classical play in a 19th-century building, one can feel the diachronic link that stretches back to the 18th century or even earlier, and helps to connect that with the 21st century. This sort of theatre building demands that theatregoing itself includes a 'time travel' orientation. The audience feels the red plush and the cornice, and we go back in time to when life was more theatrical – and more decorated! Playing in such theatres, I remember marvelling at the beauty of the intimate dress circle, as if the audience there were on stage with me, winking on the same eyeline as the actors. Somehow modern materials in modern buildings do not age well, so you get the slight faded shabbiness of the once new.

When I started out, we 'young 'uns' would be banished to a communal, shabby dressing room miles from the stage. These days, once I have negotiated the stage door with the endless key-signing ritual, I often end up with the key to Dressing Room Number One, which, as tradition would have it, is usually very near the stage. This has always amused me, as a walk is often the best bridge between the real world and the world of the play.

When I first made it to the West End, my father, from Co Cork in the Republic of Ireland, came over to see me. I remember when I had been part of a few theatrical experiments, he asked me 'Why don't you do a normal play?' But on this occasion, his question was different, for the plush and gilt – or do I mean guilt? – and the finery of London's West End had obviously got to him; he simply wanted to know whether he could still wear his sports jacket, or whether he would have to dress up with a black bow tie and a dinner suit.

There is something about these old theatres in the West End that makes you think posh, so it's important to remember that they were built for all classes and all types of people, and at a time before the arrival of cinema and television when theatregoing really was a mass pursuit. Today they still welcome London's residents, as well as visitors and tourists of all sorts and from all over the world. They are part of a larger group that is actually fantastically diverse, the older buildings having been continually augmented and revitalised. The pictures in this book capture their remarkable range and flavour as well as their ghosts and their history and the people who still inhabit them. It is a truly remarkable record.

Introduction

By Susie Barson

In what other city can you see fifty theatres within two square miles? London's West End has a rich and unique collection of theatres, varied in style and size, and ranging in date across two centuries, an outstanding architectural and cultural inheritance of which Londoners can be extremely proud. This book presents a celebratory collection of images from a comprehensive photographic survey of these buildings.

The existence of so many old theatres in the West End and the reasons behind the survey both call for some explanation. Up to and through the 19th century fire was a great and ever-present risk to theatres; they regularly burned down and were generally rebuilt from scratch. Improved fire and safety regulations mean that far fewer buildings have since been lost in this way, and many ageing theatres have been repaired, refurbished and adapted, often with little readily discernible impact. Others have gone – demolished or converted – and there should be no illusion that there was ever a static golden age when change was not in the air. Over the last few years, however, pressure for more radical change within the buildings has been increasing. There are perennial questions of attendance levels and economic viability, staging costs and the recouping of investments, as well as issues of legislative change. Theatre owners need to provide better access and circulation; they also want to be able to provide improved sightlines, more comfortable seats and ambient temperatures, along with better ancillary facilities. Backstage, old machinery has become redundant and can be deemed a health and safety hazard even if it is not actually in the way. The staging of ambitious productions in spaces that were not designed for large heavy sets, with elaborate sound and light equipment, has also caused problems.

These pressures pose numerous challenges. To inform discussions about the future of London's West End theatres, it is timely to investigate and elucidate just what the buildings comprise. No less important in the face of change is the duty to provide a publicly accessible record of what the buildings are presently like, for the sake of posterity. For these reasons English Heritage undertook a photographic survey of London's West End theatres between February 2001 and August 2002, taking in fifty theatres, of which thirty-six are included in the statutory 'list' of buildings of special architectural or historic interest. The survey had access to all areas of the buildings. The result is a photographic inventory of the interiors, including front-of-house areas, leading into the auditoria, and beyond to the backstage and other hidden spaces. There are, on average, around forty photographs from each theatre, ranging from general views of the auditoria to details of artwork and decoration, and from mechanical fittings to dressing rooms. Taken together, the photographs show how these areas combine to form the elaborate envelope for the special experience that is a live performance. They will also give theatre historians, architects, theatre owners, managers and all others concerned with theatres valuable comparative visual material to inform decisions affecting the buildings. Further, the survey in its entirety will be of use to future generations, being available to the general public through the National Monuments Record, where it supplements much illuminating earlier coverage.

This book marks the completion and shares the aims of the survey. Its core is a selection of images that reveals the interiors of these awe-inspiring yet functional buildings in all their grit and glory. The photographs capture the buildings as they are at the turn of the 21st century. They illustrate how most of the theatres have survived and adapted to a hundred years or more of staged shows night after night. Some retain original stage machinery; elsewhere there is state-of-the-art equipment. Unlike other publications devoted to the theatres, this book seeks to address the buildings as functioning entities with interdependent parts, 'factories for performing in', large areas of which have, for most of us, remained mysterious and unexplored.

The aim in publishing these images is to reach a wide audience, both regular visitors to the West End theatres – including many from overseas – as well as those who might only rarely, or perhaps never, set foot inside a red-carpeted foyer or an austere 'black box' auditorium. Many who have not visited a West End theatre for a few years may be enticed back, to appreciate afresh the period decor of the public spaces in the front-of-house areas, or the structural *tour de force* of balconies stacked almost vertically one above the other up to 'the gods'. Even for theatre cognoscenti there will be surprises.

While the photographs will inform, inspire and visually delight, accompanying text provides historical, architectural and cultural context. 'Front to Back: the anatomy of the West End theatre' sets out the nature of the buildings in both physical and cultural terms, presenting a functional understanding of theatre architecture through an awareness of theatregoing experience. It then goes beyond the common experience to address the character of backstage areas.

The photographic heart of the book is set out in an order that reflects a tour of a building, not separate expositions of each building, but a single progress through a generalised or 'typical' West End theatre. A deliberately small selection of streetscapes and exteriors represents the first fleeting view of the theatre before the spectator enters the magical world inside. The experience begins properly with the foyer, where people congregate, then moves through the passages and bars, with tantalising glimpses into the auditorium. The next section explores this area, the large open public space and the interface between spectators and performers. There are views from seats to stage and vice versa, giving a sense of the *frisson* that a performer experiences on stage when facing the multitude, as well as details of seating, period decorative plasterwork and paintings. In the last section the spectator moves backstage, and into the confined spaces above and below the stage, finally leaving by the stage door. These photographs reveal those areas not normally seen by the public and, in so

doing, enter the private realms of the theatre technicians and performers, bringing these usually hidden regions into the light, and giving a rare view of the unique quality of working life in the theatre. It is a fascinating, arcane and evocative world. Tight, cramped spaces cluttered with ropes, scenery and props, utilitarian corridors, tiny windowless dressing rooms and costume wardrobes created out of leftover corners all give a sense of a workaday environment that serves many people, from dressers to electricians, as well as the world's finest professional actors.

To conclude there is a shift of tone, from exploration and celebration to exhortation and conservation. The privileged access that the photographs afford draws attention to the fragility of much significant historic fabric, and to some of the difficult practical issues surrounding the adaptation of historic buildings to changing expectations. 'Living with the Legacy' develops the theme of survival, stressing both the desire for continuity and the need for change, and identifying some of the commercial pressures faced by the owners. Alongside The Theatres Trust and local planning authorities, English Heritage has a significant role in helping to shape the continuing evolution of the West End theatres, especially given that such a large proportion are 'listed' buildings. The nature of this responsibility is set out in 'A Balancing Act: conservation, English Heritage and the West End theatres', which explains how English Heritage is engaging with questions of conservation management and maintenance. Following on from these is a short gazetteer giving essential facts about the theatres covered by the survey, including addresses, with the dates of the main building phases and the names of the principal architects. 'Listing' status and the archive file details are also recorded. The figure references for individual theatres are to be found in this gazetteer. Finally, a selection of other books and articles on the West End theatres is provided under the heading 'Further Reading', and there is a list of contact names and addresses of institutions concerned with the function, history, fabric and archives of the West End theatres.

The purpose of this book is to spread understanding and appreciation of the working buildings that are at the heart of the British theatrical industry. It is not about the people or the productions within the buildings. While it must not be forgotten that theatres come alive at night, they are never empty: managers, building maintenance staff, carpenters, electricians and cleaners – not to mention the occasional actor – are constantly hard at work preparing for the next show (often watched over by the theatre cat). They are a cheerful and devoted group, and it is thanks to them, as well as to the impresarios and investors, that the theatres continue in that use for which they were built.

Front to Back:
the anatomy of the West End theatre

by Joanna Smith

…what London attracts with the mirage of its work shining across the counties and the countries, London holds with the glamour of its leisure…
(Ford Madox Ford, *The Soul of London*)

Theatreland

London's West End theatres together form a rich assemblage borne out of a web of theatrical traditions and the impact of over a century of adaptation to changing fashions. There have been losses and periods of retrenchment, but this group of highly specialised buildings has remained at the forefront of commercial theatrical activity since the late 19th century, its dominance challenged only by the Broadway district in New York. Most of the surviving theatres were built in the 1890s, 1900s and 1920s. Of course, there were 'West End' theatres before this date, but none has survived in its entirety, though several buildings do retain earlier 19th-century parts, or occupy sites upon which much older theatres stood. Only a handful of new theatres have been added to the ensemble since the 1930s. The area broadly accepted as London's West End (Fig 1) encompasses fifty theatres, though not all – nearer forty – show the glamorous commercial productions that have long been synonymous with 'theatreland'. This group of buildings has always been architecturally diverse, both in size and style, reflecting what was being staged – plays, music hall or variety, for example. There were some difficult decades in the middle of the 20th century, and adaptive diversity has increased. Since 1945 state-subsidised opera and ballet houses, a resurrected music hall, converted 'fringe' or experimental spaces, and purpose-built 'training' theatres operated by educational institutions have all augmented the number of venues and types of performances. That said, almost all of the West End theatres conform to a basic formula, having an auditorium with tiers of seating facing a stage framed by a curtained 'proscenium' opening. Another shared characteristic of this plenitude of theatres is that they hold their greatest pleasures within; they are self-contained, inward-looking, almost nocturnal worlds based on artifice and illusion.

Seeing a Show

In 1906 a short article entitled 'A Country Cousin's Day in London' was published as part of a two-volume anthology, *Living London*.[1] The author, George Sims, and his fictional relative began with some sightseeing, at Madame Tussaud's and the Tower of London, before moving on to an orgy of theatregoing, interspersed with eating. They commenced with an afternoon performance at the Hippodrome, before progressing to the newly opened London Coliseum, where the climax of the second of the four daily shows was a spectacular 'sea piece', then to the Alhambra for some ballet and thence to the Palace to watch the short cinematic 'Biograph' presentation. They concluded at the Empire, where they observed the 'famous men' promenading in the lounge before enjoying the finale, a grand ballet. While allowing for a degree of exaggeration, this account illustrates the sheer enthusiasm for theatregoing that existed amongst Edwardians, and hints at the dazzling array of theatrical entertainment there was to be had, and not just by the middle classes.[2] Moreover, Sims's article is restricted to central London's great 'palaces of variety'. It omits any mention of the West End's numerous playhouses and their diverse fare. This ranged from operas and 'sensation' dramas, a heady mixture of incidental music, lavish *mise-en-scène* and spectacular effects that vividly re-created contemporary or historical events, to revivals of classics and new writing, including the highly popular 'society' dramas.

While the West End of London had long contained places of theatrical entertainment, including established concentrations around Drury Lane and on the Haymarket, the theatregoing that Sims describes was essentially a late-Victorian and Edwardian phenomenon that reversed an earlier Victorian drift of the moneyed classes away from

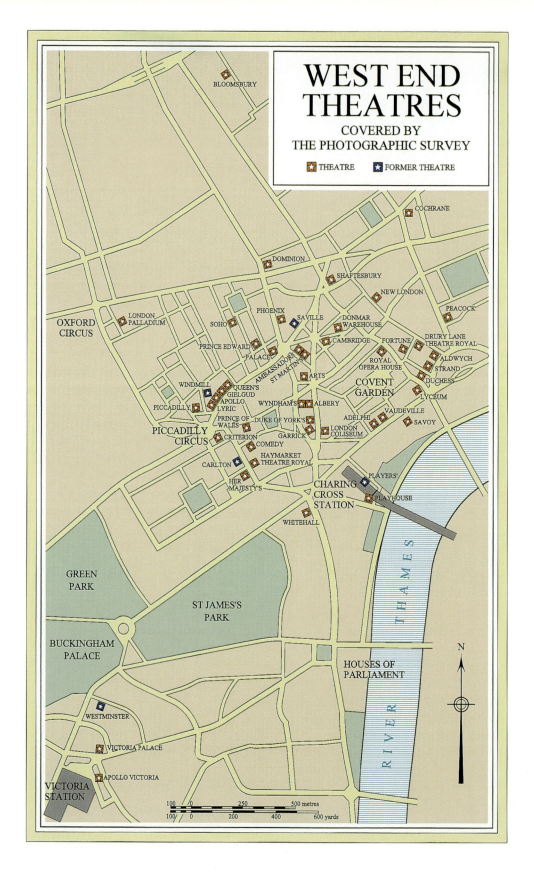

WEST END THEATRES
COVERED BY
THE PHOTOGRAPHIC SURVEY

★ THEATRE ★ FORMER THEATRE

BLOOMSBURY

COCHRANE

DOMINION

SHAFTESBURY

NEW LONDON

PEACOCK

OXFORD CIRCUS

LONDON PALLADIUM

PHOENIX

SAVILLE

DONMAR WAREHOUSE

SOHO

CAMBRIDGE

FORTUNE

DRURY LANE THEATRE ROYAL

PRINCE EDWARD

PALACE

ROYAL OPERA HOUSE

ALDWYCH

STRAND

WINDMILL

AMBASSADORS

ST MARTIN'S

ARTS

COVENT GARDEN

DUCHESS

QUEEN'S GIELGUD

APOLLO LYRIC

WYNDHAM'S

ALBERY

LYCEUM

PICCADILLY

PRINCE OF WALES

DUKE OF YORK'S

ADELPHI

VAUDEVILLE

SAVOY

PICCADILLY CIRCUS

CRITERION

GARRICK

LONDON COLISEUM

COMEDY

CARLTON

HAYMARKET THEATRE ROYAL

PLAYERS'

HER MAJESTY'S

CHARING CROSS STATION

PLAYHOUSE

WHITEHALL

THAMES

GREEN PARK

ST JAMES'S PARK

BUCKINGHAM PALACE

HOUSES OF PARLIAMENT

RIVER

N

WESTMINSTER

VICTORIA PALACE

APOLLO VICTORIA

VICTORIA STATION

100 0   250   500 metres
100 0   200   400   600 yards

theatre attendance. The causes of this change were many, not least improvements in transport and the new cultural acceptability of 'night life'. The consequence was an unprecedented boom in the building of theatres. This would not have been possible had it not been for the ending in 1843 of the monopoly of the so-called 'patent theatres', which had limited the number of venues in London legally able to stage plays. Of the fifty theatres recorded in the English Heritage survey, only three (the Royal Opera House, the Criterion and the Comedy) can be said, in substantially whole terms, to pre-date 1888, while nineteen theatres date from the boom period of 1888 to 1916. Of those others with complex histories of rebuilding and alteration, many have interiors that were reworked in the decades immediately before and after 1900.

The concentration of new venues in the West End in the mid- to late 19th century had its own momentum, tied up with the area's evolving fashionableness, with its plethora of shops, restaurants, hotels and gentlemen's clubs. Moreover, as living standards rose, and leisure time increased, the numerous attractions of the area were brought within the reach of an ever-larger number of people. The new playhouses were concentrated around new or improved streets such as Shaftesbury Avenue, Charing Cross Road, the Strand and Aldwych, sometimes grouped so closely together – most notably at the Lyric, Apollo, Gielgud and Queen's – as to form an almost continuous row (Fig 2). Most of the new theatres were built on small, constricted sites, the Palace and the London Coliseum being exceptions. But this did not inhibit the success of the playhouses. Their achievement was matched by a parallel rise to respectability of the music hall, in the guise of the variety theatre, which further extended the possibilities for the well-heeled theatregoer.

Figure 1 (facing page) Map of the West End showing the theatres covered by the photographic survey of 2001–2.

Figure 2 (right) Shaftesbury Avenue: the heart of theatreland. [AA033664]

One consequence of the late-Victorian and Edwardian theatre-building boom was the emergence of specialist architects. The first of these was C J Phipps, rapidly followed by Frank Matcham and W G R Sprague, all of whom designed almost nothing but theatres. Along with Thomas Verity and Walter Emden, these architects benefited from abundant opportunity and certainty of purpose, based on clear understandings of client needs, as well as the kinds of audiences and types of shows to be accommodated. They brought the building type to a peak of

Figure 3 W G R Sprague's glorious auditorium of 1903 in the Albery Theatre, viewed from the grand circle. [AA025673]

refinement (Fig 3). The most successful of these architects was Frank 'You can't match 'im' Matcham, who, from 1879 onwards, was responsible for more than 150 theatres all over the country, many of them serving the large variety-theatre circuits. Matcham designed four West End variety palaces from scratch, of which two continue in theatrical use, the London Coliseum and the Victoria Palace. His alterations at the London Palladium also survive.[3] The work of Sprague has fared better. He was responsible for some of the finest West End playhouses, and buildings by him of the period 1899 to 1916 include

Wyndham's, the Albery, the Aldwych, the Strand, New Ambassadors and St Martin's.

Other key elements in the formation of the 'West End show', and its associations with expense, spectacle or glamour, were the 'star' actor and the long-running production. From the late 19th century London was the hub of theatre-making, and new shows were premiered that were better staged and capable of being viewed in greater elegance and comfort than ever before. By all these means theatre owners and actor-managers were able to establish the West End show as a 'brand', further exploited and reinforced by provincial and overseas tours. A measure of their success is the fact that this 'brand' retains its currency to the present day.

In the 20th century, during the years between the First and Second World Wars, popular tastes shifted to newer forms of mass entertainment, but the West End was sustained by its proven strengths. This permitted a flourish of theatre-building in around 1930, ranging from the vast Dominion to the tiny Duchess, along with the reworking of several existing theatres. On the whole there was retrenchment to cater to smaller, more sophisticated audiences. As cinema came into vogue, theatres were increasingly provided with projection boxes. It was the music halls and variety theatres that bore the brunt of changing public tastes. The result was often conversion or replacement. A hybrid that accommodated both types of entertainment was developed, the most notable West End example of the cine-variety theatre being the Apollo Victoria. These buildings were the work of a new generation of specialist designers, some of whom had trained as, or were initially established as, theatre architects. They included Bertie Crewe, Frank Verity (the son of Thomas Verity), Edward Albert Stone and Robert Cromie.

The challenges to the commercial theatre in the period following the Second World War were of a different kind, being principally embodied in the emergence of state-subsidised national theatre, opera and ballet, and the rejection of traditional approaches to theatre architecture. In central London the construction of new venues occurred mainly on and around the South Bank and in the City, with few additions in the West End, exceptions being the Cochrane, Royalty (now Peacock), Bloomsbury and New London theatres. While most new theatre buildings attempted to update a traditional arrangement, some strove to create a different type of space, integrating the audience and stage by removing the proscenium arch. If traditional West End theatres were excoriated as 'draughty, gilded miniature opera houses'[4] ill suited to the needs of the times, the shows were enlivened by the abolition of state censorship in 1968, extending the limits of the permissible and commercially viable.

In the 1970s the strengthening conservation movement began to voice its concerns about the rate of demolition and widespread underappreciation of the West End's ageing theatres. This was reflected in the Save London's Theatres campaign and the establishment of The Theatres Trust. As the rate of loss was stemmed, focus turned to restoration, modernisation and bringing theatres back into use, resulting in significant successes in the 1990s, as in the restoration of the fire-damaged Savoy and the reopening of the Lyceum. The commercial West End theatre endures while tourism flourishes, benefiting from a blurring of the boundaries between mainstream theatre, the experimental fringe and the subsidised theatre, as well as cinema and television, with influences flowing in all directions.

A Gorgeous Advertisement

The typical late-Victorian or Edwardian theatre is made up of three distinct areas: first, the entrance foyers, bars and circulation areas, known as the front of house, which strictly also incorporates the auditorium, though that is here regarded as a second area; third is the backstage, which includes the stage itself. This tripartite separation has remained the norm in the West End. Furthermore, there is a clear split,

both functionally and spatially, between the backstage and the front of house, with the resident populations of each side seeming rarely to cross the divide. Those areas dedicated to public use are, inevitably, the most highly decorated. Well out of view are other spaces, such as staff offices and, when first built, accommodation for owners or managers, as at the Vaudeville and Her Majesty's. Such facilities were commonly located in the upper levels or to the sides of the front half of the theatre.

Of the several factors that influenced the design and appearance of the West End theatre, the key consideration was the financial need to lure and accommodate large numbers of people in comfort and safety in an almost invariably small available space. The strategy of enticement began with the exterior, which typically sought to combine architectural dignity with a touch of frivolity, though impact was often constrained by cramped sites and limited frontages. The grouping together of theatres, as where the Strand and Aldwych theatres flanked the Waldorf Hotel, allowed for greater effect. A variety of styles was deployed, including the Flemish Renaissance, art nouveau and neo-Baroque, but seldom purely applied. As Sprague explained: 'I like the Italian Renaissance for the frontages, but modify and take liberties that no architect would ever demur so as to get the best effects.'[5] Nor was the external style always carried through to the interior; Sprague favoured an elegant rococo or French treatment for his auditoria. In their wonderfully eclectic façades and interiors the theatre specialists used oversized keystones, mixed up the Classical orders, and played with the proportions of column and pilaster shafts. Figure sculpture added to the sense of knowing indiscipline. The theatre architects were at a slight remove from the mainstream of contemporary architectural practice, a factor in their subsequent underappreciation.

Economic imperatives meant that the auditorium took as large a share as possible of the building volume. Given the constraints of small sites ingenious planning was required to fit anterooms into the

Figure 4 The social hierarchy of the auditorium, graphically expressed in the Lyceum Theatre in the sudden disappearance of decoration over the highest, and cheapest, tier of seats. [AA032770]

remaining space, flexibility being further circumscribed by the necessary provision of passages to fire exits. Moreover, a hierarchical division of public spaces was required in order to give wealthier theatregoers the best entrances, finest bars and, ideally, the shortest travelling distance to their seats. For this section of the audience, the theatre architect turned spatial limitations to advantage, creating intimate areas that could be elegantly decorated and placed so as to form a sequence from entrance to auditorium, setting the mood for the delights to come. These anterooms were given chandeliers, picture- or mirror-hung walls and cosy fireplaces, all seen to best advantage after dusk, in keeping with the nocturnal nature of theatre use. Further, their domestic scale magnified the impact of the comparatively vast auditorium. The less affluent theatregoer was also subjected to this manipulation of scale, though in a starker manner, having perhaps entered the theatre from a side door, thence being either funnelled into the 'pit' at the rear of the stalls,

or forced to make the long climb up spartan stairways to the plainly treated upper balcony and its bench seating (Fig 4).

Once seated, the concerns of the expectant audience could be summarised as: 'Can I see well, can I hear well, shall I be comfortable, shall I be safe, and will the decorations be agreeable?'[6] If commercial considerations and artifice were paramount they had to be tempered by regard for structural safety, fireproofing, sanitation and ventilation. By the 1890s, legislative requirements – codified in various building acts and regulations that were enforced with increasing vigilance[7] – were having a clear impact on theatre design. Safety was a critical issue at this time since many theatres were destroyed by fire; the average life expectancy of a London theatre was estimated at a mere twenty-one years in the 1880s.[8] The London County Council set up a theatres committee, and the subject even merited the attention of a Government Select Committee in 1892. The technical press of the day proffered numerous articles about theatre construction and fire prevention.

One way in which some of both legal and audience requirements could be met was by the application of new building technologies. The form of auditorium that developed in the early 19th century required slender cast-iron columns to support the tiers of seating, a visually intrusive arrangement that survives at the Criterion and Comedy theatres. The introduction of more versatile wrought-iron structural members from the 1850s, and steel cantilevers from the 1880s, permitted the construction of deeper balconies with greater seating capacity and reduced dependence on intermediate supporting columns.[9] Used most dramatically at the Palace Theatre, this technology gave larger numbers of people better views, though the hierarchical nature of the theatres required that the best sightlines should continue to be from the first-balcony or dress-circle seats. Fully column-free balcony construction in steel, breathtakingly exploited by Matcham at the London Coliseum, was a feature of almost all auditoria after 1900.

Another consequence of safety concerns had been the virtual separation of the auditorium from the backstage by a fireproof wall rising from the foundations to the roof, the division being made complete by a safety curtain in the stage opening, sometimes of iron construction, and iron doors to any other openings. This need for segregation contributed to the retreat of the stage behind the proscenium wall, the necessarily closable opening being readily set within its own frame, thereby creating the illusion of the stage as a picture. This frame was usually edged by, and in some instances formed from, tiers of boxes, offering privileged visibility to and from the audience rather than to the stage. At least one of these boxes was designated by custom as the 'royal box', with its own anteroom or retiring room and sometimes its own entrance.

Initially these boxes were used by the Prince of Wales, later King Edward VII, and other family members, but not by Queen Victoria, who had ceased to attend the theatre after Prince Albert's death. Other late 19th-century innovations that enhanced the comfort and safety of wealthier patrons included the introduction of fixed 'tip-up' upholstered seating, individually numbered and therefore capable of being reserved in advance.

As for the decoration, this was provided by specialist teams of artists and craftsmen who adorned the entrance foyers, bars, passages and auditoria with painted and gilded plaster decoration; sculpture in plaster, wood and bronze; marble fireplaces; oil paintings and *trompe l'œil* mural paintings; and illusionistic or abstract painted safety curtains, the subjects depicted ranging from Antique myths to Shakespearian scenes. Such decorative 'superabundance' has been much denigrated, and so it was even before its heyday; in 1859 George Augustus Sala mocked 'The style of decoration in which the Louis Quinze contends with the Arabesque, and that again with the Cockney Corinthian…'.[10] In fact, much of the ornamentation, if not always overarchingly coherent or sophisticated in its execution, was skilfully gauged through an understanding of what would be visible and appear luxurious at a distance in subdued lime-, gas- or candlelight. The new respectability of theatregoing required appropriately ornate auditoria, able to 'produce an atmosphere of opulent comfort and to excite expectancy'.[11] But there was no single approach to the treatment of these spaces, which ranged from the heavy red-plush and gilt interiors of the variety palaces to the lighter, more delicate decorative schemes of the playhouses. What they shared was an ornamental approach, in paint or plaster, which revelled in its superficiality.

The auditoria of the 20th-century inter-war theatres also sought to be places that gratified and excited the senses of the audience, though the sleeker decorative styles of the day provided a marked contrast with what had gone before. Electric lighting, first used at

Figure 5 A swathe of tip-up seating in the Adelphi Theatre's stalls, viewed from the upper circle. [BB009728]

the Savoy in 1881, had become the norm, enabling brighter, safer, less stuffy and more variably lit theatres. The impact of cinema design was felt in a new generation of playhouses such as the Fortune, the Cambridge and the reconstructed Savoy, triumphs of art-deco styling. Trends towards a diminishing number of boxes and 'arena' seating were also consequences of cinema.

In theatres built after the Second World War 'honesty' was often substituted for 'magic', as decoration was minimised or abolished. The technical 'guts' of the theatre were left on show and the seating arrangements aimed for egalitarianism and flexibility. Such experimentation was in part prompted by a desire to take theatre back to its historical roots, stripping illusion down to its most fundamental forms. The resulting 'black box' auditorium, with fixed seating around three sides of a floor-level acting area, can be seen at the Donmar Warehouse and the Soho. The most innovative late 20th-century space in the West End is to be found at the New London, which is equipped with a revolving stage and a non-structural, and therefore, removable proscenium.

Technological revolutions in lighting and sound have also left their marks on older auditoria, with obtrusive equipment awkwardly attached to balcony fronts, on inserted bridges that span the auditorium, or colonising the side boxes. Other changes have included the removal of 'pit' benches at the back of the stalls, and the redundancy of many orchestra pits, allowing the serried rows of seating (Fig 5), whether staggered, aligned in solid blocks or segmented by aisles, to sweep out from under the balcony right up to the stage front.

Behind the Scenes

Like the front of house, the backstage is made up of several different areas that can, in the largest theatres, be almost equivalent in size. At the heart is the stage, a place of heightened sensations and ordered jumble when set up for a performance, little more than a black-painted void when not. Ranged above and below are more mysterious regions, the domain of technical staff. The backstage has also to accommodate dressing rooms and, to varying degrees, dedicated spaces for sets, props, costumes and wigs. The character of the whole is in marked contrast to the public spaces, being generally stark and functional, shabby and notably unglamorous, though often personalised by the occupants. Despite ageing building fabric and minimal comforts, these areas hold a strong romantic appeal for those who work in and visit them. Indeed, the contrast between the outward show on stage and the backstage environment in which it is created is a key characteristic of the theatre ethos (Fig 6). For outsiders, for whom the backstage regions are usually out of bounds, these spaces hold the compelling fascination of the forbidden and unknown.

General unfamiliarity with the backstage world is not new. Despite the popularity of theatregoing, few Victorian writers felt obliged to visit the backstage

Figure 6 Though almost empty, the stage at the Bloomsbury Theatre is 'ready'. It is viewed here from the side, which is cluttered with lighting rigs, scenery flats and other equipment. [AA032826]

in print. A notable and early exception was Sala, whose account of theatres in 1859 included 'those charmed regions which lie beyond the stage-door'.[12] He used the daily ebb and flow of activity within the theatre to draw out the different backstage occupations in turn. More detailed expositions of how these areas functioned were produced in the late 19th century, as theatre-building boomed, but these were essentially technical.[13] This reluctance to describe the backstage world may have been influenced by then-current notions of gentility or propriety, which meant that those likely to be reading accounts of theatres should not be interested in areas 'below stairs'.[14] It ensured that the increasingly spectacular stage illusions that were the consequence of new developments in lighting and stage machinery

retained their mystery for late-Victorian and Edwardian audiences. Perhaps then, as now, commentators shared with performers and crew the sense that backstage activities were 'somehow secret and not to be seen by outsiders'.[15]

One part of the backstage is the 'stagehouse', usually formed of three elements, the 'fly tower', rising often to a considerable height, the stage itself, and an understage that might, if of several levels, descend to an almost equivalent depth. This arrangement was refined in the late 19th century to facilitate more impressive stage effects and smoother scene changes. The purpose of the tower was to enable sets to be suspended above the stage, hung under a 'lantern' from a structure known as the 'grid', from where they

Figure 7 Located high above the stage, the wooden 'grid' of the New Ambassadors Theatre, with drum- and shaft-lifting mechanism. [AA025980]

could be 'flown' down to the stage. Alternatively they could be dropped through 'cuts' in the stage floor to the space below. This activity was controlled from high-level galleries or 'fly floors' spanning the walls on the side of the stage. The understage might have two levels: the upper, referred to as the 'mezzanine', housed the 'bridges,' which could raise or lower sections of the stage, or operate a variety of smaller openings called 'traps' that were used by the performers; the lower space, the 'cellar', housed the machinery for these operations. Bulky equipment for sound and lighting effects had also to be accommodated within the stagehouse.

Stage machinery in late 19th-century theatres was the product of a gradual evolution of traditional technology, such as rope or 'hemp lines', and wooden drums and shafts for heavy lifting, all powered manually. From the 1880s, however, hydraulic power began to be used, usually for raising the weighty new safety curtains, but in some cases, as at the Drury Lane Theatre Royal and the Lyric, to power the stage bridges.[16] Thereafter, the introduction of electric motors soon provided an alternative means of power that was preferred for later innovations such as stage revolves, like the famous 'triple revolve' installed in the London Coliseum in 1904. Counterweighted flying systems had also begun to appear in the late 19th century; they were provided as part of the advanced stage machinery in the Palace Theatre in 1891. These have been widely adopted, though traditional hand-hauled methods still continue in some theatres, as at the New Ambassadors. Changing production requirements in the later part of the 20th century have often rendered the understage an underused space, perhaps given over to workshops or storage or simply left empty.

Perhaps the most striking thing about the typical 'Edwardian' stagehouse is the persistence of traditional forms of construction. It remained a predominantly wooden world up to the 1920s (Fig 7). This was in marked contrast to the application of new building technologies in the auditorium, and can in part be credited to the status and conservative tenacity of the stage carpenter and stage machinist. It was they, and not the architects, who were responsible for the design of these areas. Their artisan traditionalism was dismissed as 'antediluvian' by those who wished to see the application of more up-to-date materials. Backstage staff rarely wield design power today, but theirs remains a highly specialised field with its own particular expertise and vocabulary, still littered with arcane terms: sloats, cuts and corsican traps; double- or single-purchase flying systems; cloths, drops and house tabs.[17]

All the surviving pre-1920 stagehouses have undergone incremental change or renewal, but a surprising amount of original or early stage machinery has survived, often obsolescent and left *in situ* only because removal would have involved unnecessary expenditure. The impact of health and safety legislation and the need for broader modernisation is bringing about transformations of the older backstage areas. Renewal is of the essence in the history of West End theatres. Yet, as the theatre historian George Rowell has observed:

Caught up in the urgency of its fortunes, the theatre today, as always, is concerned principally with the present. It may dream of the future, but has no time for the past. Nevertheless, the past is part of the same design as the present, and the future will be fashioned from both.[18]

1 Sims, George R (ed) 1906. *Living London,* vol II. London: Cassell & Co.

2 According to the Baedeker guide London possessed 65 theatres and about 500 music halls in 1892, with a combined annual attendance of around 100 million. *See* Baedeker, Karl 1892. *London and its Environs.* Leipzig: Baedeker, 40.

3 Matcham's Hippodrome (1900) has been much altered internally and the Winter Garden (1911) has been demolished.

4 Wrede, Caspar 1960. 'New wine in old bottles'. *The London Magazine*, July 1960, as reprinted in *The Theatres Trust Newsletter*, no. 64, June 2002, 8–9.

5 *The Era*, November 1902, 15.

6 *The Sketch*, 5 May 1897, quoted in Maguire, Hugh, 'The architectural response', *in* Foulkes 1992, 54.

7 The Metropolitan Board of Works inspected all places of entertainment after 1878, though its powers of enforcement were limited to music halls. These powers were pursued more vigorously from 1882. The London County Council regulations on theatres were published in 1892.

8 Buckle, James George 1884. *Building and Engineering News*, 12 January 1884, 18.

9 For the constructional context see Clarke, Jonathan 2000. 'Early structural steel in London buildings', English Heritage Architectural Survey report in the National Monuments Record.

10 Sala, George Augustus 1859. *Twice Round the Clock.* London, 243.

11 Earl, John, 'London theatres', *in* Walker 1980, 60.

12 Sala, George Augustus 1859. *Twice Round the Clock.* London, 236.

13 *See* the list of Further Reading for details of accounts by James George Buckle, Ernest A E Woodrow and Edwin O Sachs.

14 Booth, Michael R 1981. *Victorian Theatrical Trades.* London: Society for Theatre Research, vii.

15 Callow, Simon 2001. 'Smoke and mirrors', *The Guardian Weekend*, 12 May 2001, 41.

16 The hydraulic bridges at the Lyric were removed to allow for the installation of a stage revolve.

17 For explanations of these terms *see* Reid 1995.

18 Rowell, George 1978. *The Victorian Theatre 1792–1914: A Survey.* Cambridge: Cambridge University Press, 149–50.

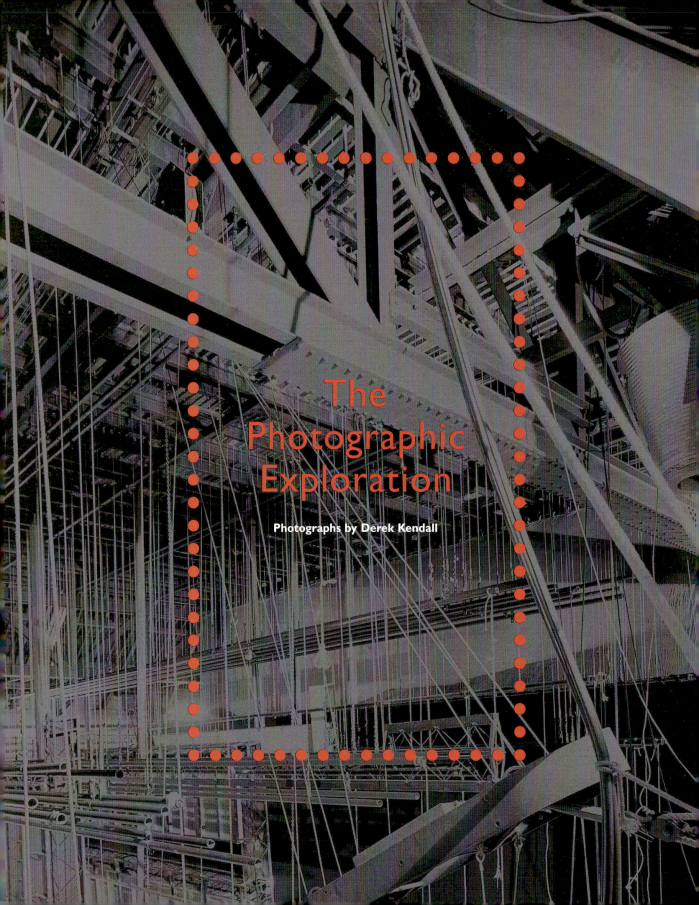

The Photographic Exploration

Photographs by Derek Kendall

The arrangement of the photographs here follows the tripartite arrangement of the West End theatres. Rather than illustrations of each building in turn, what is presented is a visual tour, in which most of the buildings recorded in the survey are represented. This tour commences at the public entrance and exits at the stage door, exploring *en route* the types of spaces that make up the theatres. Some of these areas, and the activities that occur in them, will be familiar to theatregoers, others less so. One purpose is to emphasise and balance the dual aspects of the buildings, the public front of house – though here, too, there are little-seen spaces – and the private backstage. The thematic approach also draws out the sheer variety of style, size and decoration. Different approaches to surface ornamentation, the impact of changing fashions in staging, and the workaday detail of functional aspects are all present in these images. The photographs also try to capture something of the artifice and illusion that is fundamental to a working theatre. Because these illustrations are primarily intended as a record of the buildings the images are mostly unpeopled, thereby allowing the theatres to, as it were, take centre stage.

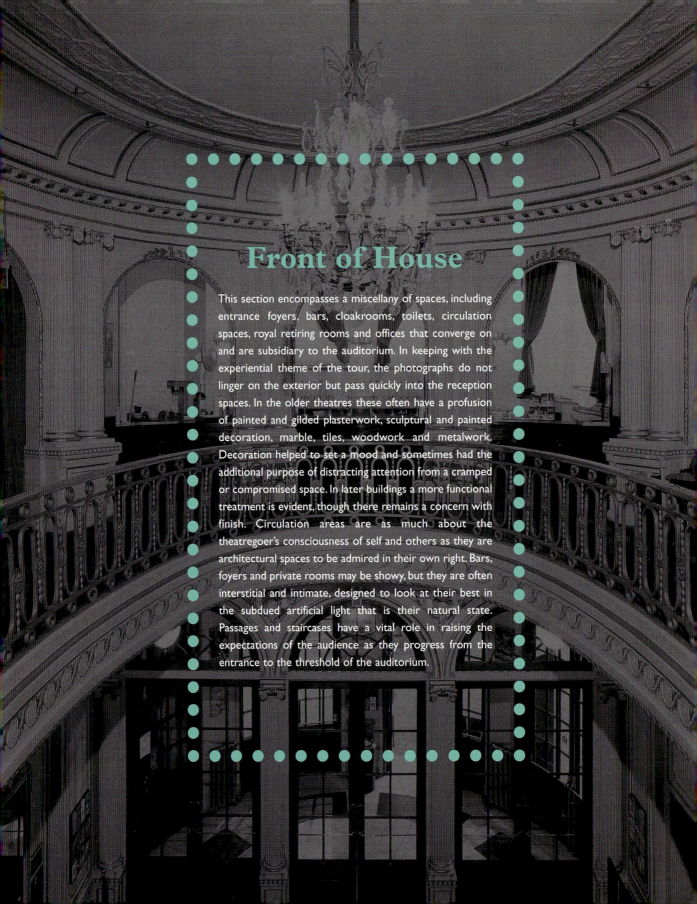

Front of House

This section encompasses a miscellany of spaces, including entrance foyers, bars, cloakrooms, toilets, circulation spaces, royal retiring rooms and offices that converge on and are subsidiary to the auditorium. In keeping with the experiential theme of the tour, the photographs do not linger on the exterior but pass quickly into the reception spaces. In the older theatres these often have a profusion of painted and gilded plasterwork, sculptural and painted decoration, marble, tiles, woodwork and metalwork. Decoration helped to set a mood and sometimes had the additional purpose of distracting attention from a cramped or compromised space. In later buildings a more functional treatment is evident, though there remains a concern with finish. Circulation areas are as much about the theatregoer's consciousness of self and others as they are architectural spaces to be admired in their own right. Bars, foyers and private rooms may be showy, but they are often interstitial and intimate, designed to look at their best in the subdued artificial light that is their natural state. Passages and staircases have a vital role in raising the expectations of the audience as they progress from the entrance to the threshold of the auditorium.

From the outside

Figure 8 (above) Signage on the Westminster Theatre, on the fringe of the West End. This theatre was extensively rebuilt and clad in Welsh slate in 1965–6. It closed in 2002. [AA025988]

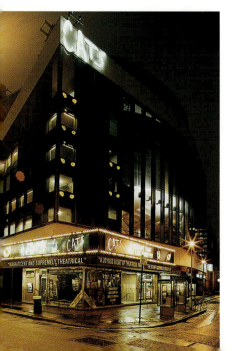

Figure 9 (above) The close proximity and long history of theatres in Covent Garden is reflected here. Part of the façade of 1811–12 to the Drury Lane Theatre Royal is seen in the glass walling to the Royal Opera House's Floral Hall extension of 1997–9. [AA033184]

Figure 10 (left) The New London Theatre, the home of *Cats* for 21 years up to 2002, is one of the West End's newest theatres. In this night view the curved back of the 'egg-in-a-box' auditorium can be seen projecting over the staircases up from the entrance foyer. [AA032021]

Figure 11 (below) Since 1903 the best entrance to the Savoy Theatre has been from a short court off the Strand that leads to the Savoy Hotel alongside. Glass, gilt and stainless steel shimmer in an elevation that was modified in 1929. [AA032930]

Figure 12 (right) A detail of the main entrance doors to the Duchess Theatre. [AA020290]

The way in

Figure 13 (above) The ample foyer at the London Palladium, a sumptuous transitional space, dedicated to giving those who could afford the better seats a feeling of grandeur and occasion *en route* to the stalls and dress circle. [AA020445]

Figure 14 (left) A disused box office just inside the entrance to Wyndham's Theatre. Though small it is embellished as befits what was the main pay box. [AA025748]

Figure 15 (right) A view from inside the Victoria Palace Theatre, looking out through the bevelled glass panes of the inner doors. [AA032443]

Figure 16 (above) The jazzy entrance foyer of the Whitehall Theatre. [AA025523]

Figure 17 (above) The more imposing entrance foyer to Her Majesty's Theatre. Herbert Beerbohm Tree, who built this theatre, is commemorated by an inscribed stone on the back wall. [AA020563]

Figure 18 (left) Advertising the last performance at the Westminster Theatre. [AA025991]

Figure 19 (above) Many theatres have 'Hall of Fame' or equivalent displays in front-of-house spaces, chronicling the great actors and productions that have passed through. Here, at the London Palladium, photographs are accompanied by a bust of Sir Edward Moss, who, with Sir Oswald Stoll, founded Moss Empires Ltd in 1899 to undertake a range of theatre enterprises, not just in the West End, but also across the country. [AA020486]

Figure 20 (above) The Gielgud Theatre was renamed in 1994 in honour of Sir John Gielgud. This view from the balconied dress-circle bar down to the main entrance emphasises the importance of Edwardian front-of-house circulation spaces for seeing and being seen – not the show, that is, but other theatregoers. [AA025561]

Figure 21 (left) A commemorative plaque in the entrance foyer of the Fortune Theatre, with a designed public ashtray. [AA032301]

Figure 22 (left) The front of the modest Arts Theatre at street level was remodelled in 2001 to be a café open to all passers-by, not just theatregoers, a means of bringing the establishment additional income all through the day. [AA032211]

Figure 23 (below) Inside the New London Theatre, up the stairs from the entrance foyer, and within the glass envelope of the front wall (see Fig 10), this viewpoint is under the upper rows of seats. In traditional manner, though in a Modernist idiom, a processional route flatters the theatregoer's visibility and self-awareness. [AA032024]

Circulation

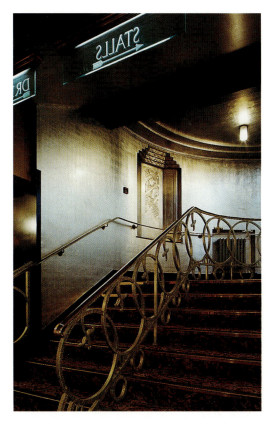

Figure 24 (above) The art-deco interiors of the Savoy Theatre are faithful reproductions of those of 1929 by Basil Ionides, destroyed in a devastating fire in 1990, but retrieved by 1993 through the work of Whitfield Partners. Gold and silver are throughout dominant colours, as here, where stairs lead down from the entrance foyer to the stalls. [AA032933]

Figure 25 (right) This ushers' telephone, linked to the box office and the upper-circle pay box, but long disused, is on a landing of the stairs up to the upper circle at the Haymarket Theatre Royal. It highlights the disconnected complexity of front-of-house spaces. [AA032922]

Figure 26 (above) This view from dress-circle level at the Palace Theatre shows the classical grandeur of the principal staircase, and the distance that has to be climbed to reach the upper tiers. [AA020769]

Figure 27 (above) The Criterion Theatre of 1873–4 is, in West End terms, an important early survival. It was London's first wholly below-ground theatre; the exploitation of excavated space became a distinctive feature of West End theatres, to make the most expensive seats in the dress circle the most accessible. These decorative tiles by Messrs Simpson and Sons from a remodelling of 1883–4 include the names of composers, reflecting the Criterion's early use for operettas. [AA032178]

Figure 28 (above) The higher the climb and the cheaper the seats, the humbler the decoration. Yet there is simple and practical elegance in the tiled walls of this staircase to the upper circle of the Victoria Palace Theatre. [AA032452]

Figure 29 (above) Prominent at the base of the staircase from the entrance foyer of St Martin's Theatre is this low-relief portrait memorial to Meggie Albanesi, 'an artist who died in the service of the theatre' in 1923. [AA032845]

Figure 30 (above) The restored vestibule from the Charing Cross Road entrance of the Phoenix Theatre has a frieze with a Latin inscription that commemorates those responsible for the building. [AA025614]

Figure 31 The earliest, and grandest, theatre interiors in the West End are the front-of-house spaces at the Drury Lane Theatre Royal, from the rebuilding of 1811–12. The imperial-pattern Prince's Stair sweeps theatregoers up, offering views on the way of the neoclassical 'rotunda' beyond. [AA020355]

Figure 32 (above) Early bar fittings are rare in West End theatres, such facilities tending to need and to receive upgrading at frequent intervals. This piece of bar-fitting is in the notably small New Ambassadors Theatre. [AA025962]

Figure 33 (right) The grand saloon in the Drury Lane Theatre Royal forms part of an early 19th-century front-of-house ensemble (see Fig 31). Fine classical decor aside, it is the scale of this room that sets it apart in what is the grandest of West End theatres. [AA020354]

• • • • • • • • • • • **Bars**

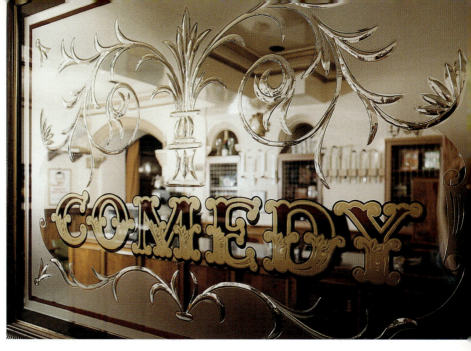

Figure 34 (above) The stalls bar in the Strand Theatre, with its ironwork and dark wood, is an archetypal Edwardian theatre bar. [AA032958]

Figure 35 (above) Redolent of a pub – a cut-glass mirror in the stalls bar of the Comedy Theatre. [AA025360]

Figure 36 (below) Bars were among the last facilities to be tucked into the interstices of intricately laid out West End theatres, space for the auditoria being at a premium. The circle bar at the Prince of Wales Theatre nestles under the rake of a balcony. [AA020843]

Figure 37 (left) This view from the head of the main staircase in the Aldwych Theatre looks across to the dress-circle bar and back down to the entrance. Circulation areas and bars are often integrated to make the most of what little space is available. [AA032700]

Figure 38 (right) This decorative glass panel behind the circle bar at the Peacock Theatre depicts a royal coach, a reference to the theatre's original name – the Royalty. [AA032414]

Figure 39 (below) The commodious upper-circle bar of the Garrick Theatre, showing the plush grandeur, more gentleman's club than pub, that aimed to lure the late-Victorian middle classes back to theatregoing. [AA020238]

Private spaces

Figure 40 (left) Private retiring rooms have *en suite* toilet facilities, as here in the Aldwych Theatre. These are better finished than those elsewhere in the theatre, and are less likely to have been refurbished. [AA032710]

Figure 41 (left) The art-deco opulence of the Savoy Theatre is sustained in its Royal Reception Room. Royal boxes, private retiring rooms and independent entrances were designed to permit eminent theatregoers to come and go without having to endure direct contact with the multitudes. [AA032942]

Figure 42 (right) This view of a royal reception room water closet, at the London Coliseum, is perhaps reminiscent of an idea of the inside of a royal train. The original royal box of 1904 was, in fact, reached via a moving carriage placed on rails that ran from the front door to the auditorium. [AA025403]

Figure 43 A rehearsal area is a rare and envied luxury in West End theatres. It is all the more desirable in a venue committed to new writing, so the Soho Theatre was designed with this simple upper-storey space for rehearsals. [AA025444]

Figure 44 (below) The building of a new stagehouse for the Royal Opera House in 1997–9 provided the opportunity for the creation of state-of-the-art rehearsal spaces. There is a suite of ballet studios, each top lit and sound proofed, with sprung floors. [AA033232]

Figure 45 (above) Inside the dome at the top of Her Majesty's Theatre is this extraordinary space, a rehearsal studio for Herbert Beerbohm Tree's 'acting academy' that doubled as a banqueting hall. [AA020614]

Threshold ····

Figure 46 (left) A view into the auditorium of the Whitehall Theatre through the latecomers' window. [AA025529]

Figure 47 (below) This view into the Aldwych Theatre's dress circle shows some of the best seats in the house. Dress circles give the clearest views of stages. [AA032712]

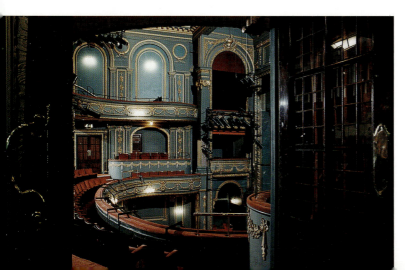

Figure 48 (above) West End theatre architects made a virtue of necessity, using the contrast between cramped circulation areas and spacious auditoria to create pre-drama drama through views from the threshold of the auditorium, as here in the Garrick Theatre's dress circle. [AA020210]

Figure 49 (above) The Bloomsbury Theatre rejects Edwardian hierarchies and fripperies with simple wrap-round circulation and more egalitarian access to the auditorium. [AA032809]

Figure 50 (right) This glass door at an entrance to the Lorenz Auditorium in the Soho Theatre carries a message of thanks, with the names of sponsors and donors whose support made the formation of this new theatre possible – a reflection of the realities of funding commercial theatre in the West End at the beginning of the 21st century. [AA025439]

Figure 51 (below) The promenade behind the royal (dress) circle at the Haymarket Theatre Royal reflects the informal and sociable nature of Edwardian theatregoing, providing, as it did, a place for convivial conversation with a screened view of the stage. [AA032898]

Figure 52 This view from Wyndham's Theatre looks through the curtained portal from which the theatregoer emerges into the stalls. [AA025703]

The Auditorium

Strictly a part of the front of house, the auditorium is, of course, central in a theatre, and is therefore treated here as a separate 'middle' section. Most West End theatres have a traditional auditorium, with one to four tiers of seating, facing a proscenium opening and the stage beyond, though other arrangements are also depicted here. In character the auditoria range between the vast and the intimate, though even the smallest can impart a sense of spaciousness. Integral to the experience in the older theatres is the decoration – often profuse and highly wrought – adorning walls, ceilings, balcony fronts and proscenia. This is sometimes carried through even to the safety curtain, a minor theatrical art form in its own right. Auditorium seating provides a multiplicity of views towards the stages, whether from a side box, the back of the stalls or the highest-level gallery, encompassing an even wider range of form and arrangement than might be expected. Another significant view, that of the auditorium from the stage, is also represented here. Many of the late-Victorian and Edwardian auditoria have undergone some alteration, seating having been reworked, decorative schemes having come and gone, and greater reliance on lighting and sound effects having had an impact. More modern buildings have usually eschewed ornament and brought the stage back into the main space. All share the same goal, to bring audience and performer together and make them feel as one.

The experience of the auditorium

Figure 53 (below) This painted plaster cherub is part of the light-fitting arrangements at the Palace Theatre, among the first theatres to be lit by electricity when it opened in 1891. [AA020779]

Figure 54 (above) A view at dress-circle level in the Playhouse Theatre, showing serpentine balcony fronts with painted balustrades in a glorious Edwardian interior. The junction between the upper balcony and the wall, decorated in the style of an 18th-century French painting, is clumsy or insouciant, according to prejudice. [AA032786]

Figure 55 (below) The Players' Theatre was the last survivor of the music-hall tradition in the West End. Created in the space underneath railway arches close to Charing Cross Station, the theatre swapped arches over the years, but the interior arrangement of a striped tented ceiling, with a bar and tables located at the back of the gallery, was retained. The theatre closed in 2002. [AA032098]

Figure 56 (above) A detail of plaster enrichment in the Playhouse Theatre, a comedy mask with musical attributes. [AA032783]

Figure 57 (above) The Strand Theatre's stalls seating, reflected in the elaborately framed mirrors on the side wall of the auditorium. Above is the dress-circle balcony front, with finely detailed swags of fruit, flowers and leaves, all part of the Edwardian decorative scheme. [AA032965]

Figure 58 (below) A view across the auditorium of St Martin's Theatre, opened in 1916 during wartime. Soberly panelled in polished hardwood, the decor is a contrast to the lightness of pre-war theatres. [AA032847]

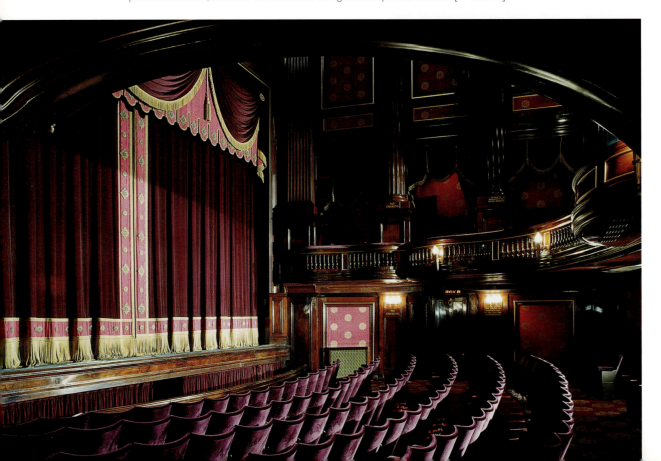

Figure 59 (right) The splendid Edwardian auditorium of the Haymarket Theatre Royal is the third in the present building, frequent rebuilding having been the norm. It has been elegantly restored, complete with boxes with draped canopies; the lighting bars are necessary for modern staging. [AA032912]

Figure 60 (below) The intimate scale of the Duchess Theatre is typical of the West End's playhouses built between the First and Second World Wars. Its circular, shallow-domed ceiling with concealed lighting is an early example of this subtle way of lighting an auditorium, much used in subsequent theatres. [AA020307]

Figure 61 (above) A view from the stage to the auditorium in the Strand Theatre, showing the fine French-style Edwardian interior. The balcony fronts step back as they go up, with the decoration becoming simpler, to reflect the hierarchy of seat prices and social classes. The boxes, which are not aligned with the balconies, are framed by a richly adorned aedicule made up of two pilasters and an entablature. [AA032984]

Figure 62 (left) The simple padded benches at stalls level and along the three-sided gallery, with extensive lighting and sound equipment on open display, give the 'black box' auditorium and stage of the Donmar Warehouse a functional aspect. [AA032167]

Figure 63 (above) The cast-iron columns supporting the Comedy Theatre's dress circle obstruct the view of the stage from certain points in the stalls. [AA025357]

Figure 64 The Apollo Victoria's set for *Starlight Express* (designed by John Napier) extended into the audience, requiring the temporary removal of the proscenium arch. Extensive scaffolding for the walkway and the lighting rigs obscured much of the original decoration, which was partially restored in 2002 after the long-running show closed. [AA032260]

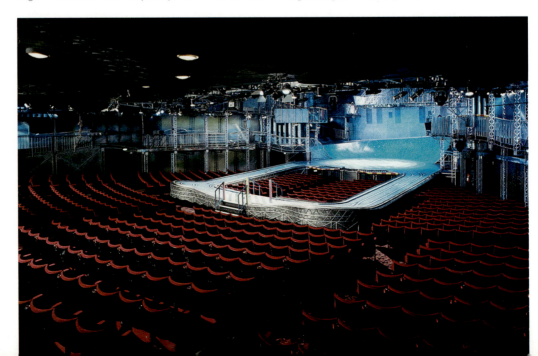

Figure 65 This view of the Comedy Theatre of 1881–4 shows the balconies supported by the slender cast-iron columns, a constructional form soon afterwards made obsolete by the use of iron-framed, and later steel-framed, cantilevered balconies, enabling unimpeded views of the stage. [AA025384]

Figure 66 A side-wall or 'slip' box in the Prince Edward Theatre, showing decorative box fronts and art-deco wall decorations. [AA020667]

Figure 67 The vaulted and panelled area to the rear of the stalls in the Palace Theatre was originally a clear unseated space, known as the 'pit', where men could stand and smoke during the musical performances. [AA020774]

Figure 68 Whitehall Theatre. [AA025541]

Figure 69 Albery Theatre. [AA025658]

Figure 70 Haymarket Theatre Royal. [AA032909]

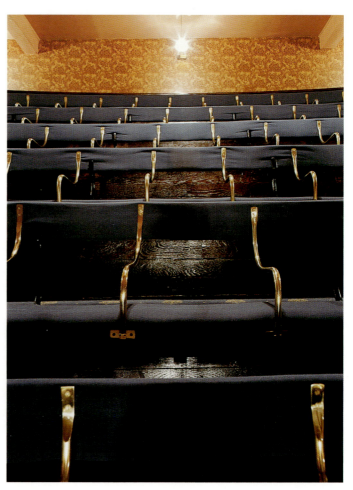

Seating
and
sightlines

Figure 71 Savoy Theatre. [AA032941]

Figure 72 Dominion Theatre. [AA032005]

Figure 73 Cochrane Theatre. [AA032347]

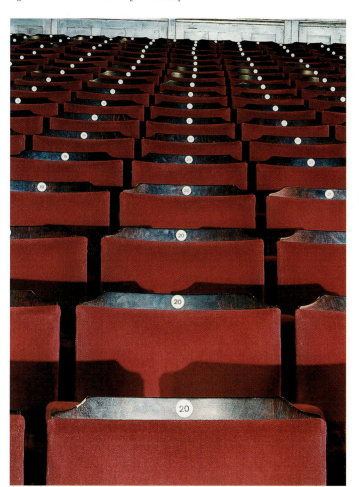

Figure 74 Padded seating has superseded the originally plain wooden benches in the Aldwych Theatre's highest tier of seating, right up in 'the gods'. The gangway divides the upper circle from the gallery, the balustrade adding security in this vertiginous part of the theatre. [AA032724]

Figure 75 A view across the deep dress circle of the London Coliseum, showing the curved, decorated soffit (underside) of the cantilevered upper-circle balcony. [AA025408]

Figure 76 A view from the back of the steeply raked circle balcony in the Piccadilly Theatre shows the painted safety curtain, depicting the statue of Eros. This celebrates the location of the theatre close to Piccadilly Circus. [AA025334]

Theatre boxes

Figure 77 (right) A view of the sumptuous decoration of the bow-fronted boxes in the grand-circle balcony of the Shaftesbury Theatre, architectural richness that warrants detailed description. Framing Ionic columns carry an entablature decorated with anthemions and wreaths, and crowned by a semicircular arch. Within the tympanum are two pedestals supporting free-standing figure sculpture, a male and female in classical dress, posed to appear to look down at the action on the stage, with attendant winged putti playing musical instruments. A pastoral scene is depicted in the painting in the lunette. [AA020736]

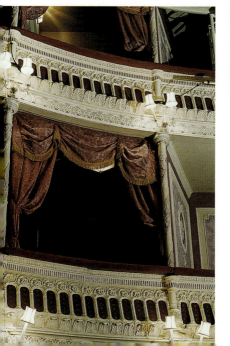

Figure 78 (left) The Criterion retains much of its late-Victorian form. This view shows the boxes, framed by slender iron columns and with balcony fronts elaborately enriched with plasterwork. The break in the box front allows sets to be carried through, a necessary device in an awkwardly planned theatre, much of which is below ground level. The rich fringed hangings are an addition. [AA032183]

Figure 79 The art-deco auditorium of the Cambridge Theatre does have a single wall-hung box, though in the 1920s and 1930s boxes were little used in theatres, which often doubled as cinemas; an oblique view of the screen was not desirable. The tympanum of the arch over the box features a Constructivist design. [AA020421]

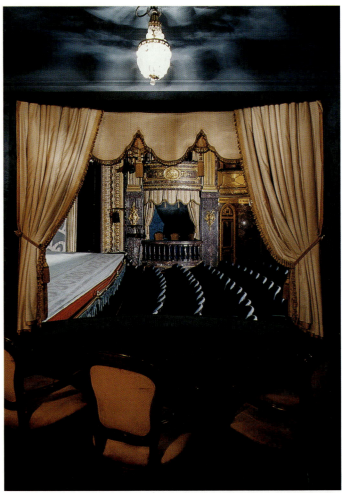

Figure 80 This view from a lower box in the Haymarket Theatre Royal illustrates the importance of seeing and being seen by others of both similar and lesser status, even at the expense of a good view of the stage. [AA032891]

Towards the stage

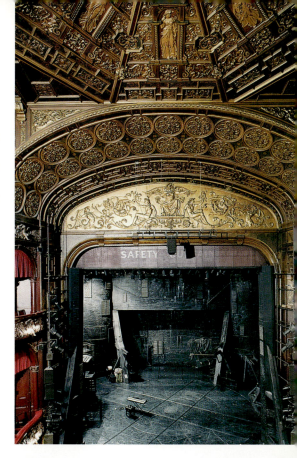

Figure 81 In front of the black void, a simple wooden proscenium arch frames the stage at the Palace Theatre, and anchors a complex sequence of planes covered in Renaissance-grotesque ornament. A tympanum leads the eye to coffered arch soffits over the boxes and on to a polygonal, compartmented ceiling, with low-relief figures in niches. [AA020783]

Figure 82 (below) The *Cats* set (designed by John Napier) in the New London Theatre provided an environment where audience and actors shared the same space, avoiding the traditional separation made by a proscenium. The production closed in 2002, soon after this photograph was taken. [AA032069]

Figure 83 Wyndham's Theatre has a good example of a 'picture-frame' proscenium, and superb house curtains, or 'tabs'. Above the arch there is a bust of Lady Wyndham, the theatre-owner's wife, flanked by roundels enclosing painted portraits of the playwright Richard Sheridan and the actor David Garrick. [AA025721]

Figure 84 The Whitehall Theatre auditorium from the back of the circle showing the chamfered proscenium arch and the geometric ceiling with concealed lighting. The restored dark colour scheme was a conscious attempt to focus attention on the stage once the play had begun, replacing the gilding of earlier auditoria with silver highlights. [AA025538]

Hidden from view

Figure 85 (right) This board controlling sound and light is temporarily located in the auditorium at the back of the London Palladium Theatre's stalls. It provides a view of the action on stage for the controller, at the expense of some loss of seats. [AA020454]

Figure 86 (below) The void above the auditorium of the Drury Lane Theatre Royal, showing the lining of the ceiling dome on the left, and an early 19th-century wooden roof truss with iron straps, reinforced by later steel trusses, all of which support both the theatre roof above and the auditorium ceiling below. [AA020384]

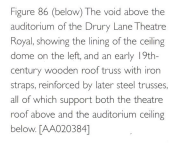

Figure 87 (above) The fire escape from the stalls to the exit in the Peacock Theatre, the stage being three storeys below ground level. [AA032416]

Figure 88 (right) An air-circulating pump of 1937 in the Prince Edward Theatre. By this date there was no longer the need to rely on 'sunburners' to draw air upwards and out of the auditorium. [AA020684]

Backstage

To move directly from the auditorium to the backstage is unusual, and often physically difficult. It is also transgressive, leaving the world of the spellbound observer to enter the world where the magic is made. The backstage area is, of course, dominated by the stage, with the understage below and the 'fly tower' above. This division of space evolved to accommodate the complex processes involved in staging a show, changing the scenery, creating spectacular effects with sets, sound and lighting, and getting the performers on and off the stage. The result is often a hotchpotch of interpenetrating layers of machinery and equipment, some of it obsolete but much still in use, which might range in date from the late-Victorian era to the present day. The geography and terminology of the backstage are complex: where, for example, is the 'fly floor' and what happens there? The stage itself may be formed of several parts that can be raised, lowered or revolved, under the control of machinery located in the understage. High above the stage is the 'grid', the lattice of metal or wood from which sets and cloths are suspended, moved or 'flown', usually from a gallery on the side wall (the 'fly floor'). The backstage has other functions to accommodate, however, including dressing rooms for the actors, workshops for the carpenters and electricians, and, in some theatres, dedicated spaces for building or storing sets, props and costumes. Most of these areas are as characteristically plain as the front-of-house areas can be ornate. Black voids, poky corridors and seemingly formless spaces with ramshackle machines can, however, elicit their own considerable charm and fascination.

Around the stage: lighting, traps and props

Figure 89 (right) A diaphanous backcloth, here seen from behind, hides the back wall of the Arts Theatre's stage from view and forms the back of the set. The seats are stored out of the way until required for the next performance. [AA032229]

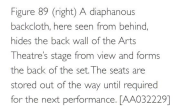

Figure 90 (left) As a result of heavy wear the carpets in the front of house have to be regularly replaced, though the carpet design may change less frequently. Here in the Drury Lane Theatre Royal, carpet sections for the Really Useful Theatre Group are being machined by hand by Brian Byeworth, using specialised equipment. [AA020399]

Figure 91 (left) Before electronic amplification was available ingenious methods had to be devised to create sound effects. Shaking this sheet of metal, in the Vaudeville Theatre, simulated the sound of thunder. [AA032146]

Figure 92 (right) Lighting sets in store on the rear stage area in the Peacock Theatre. [AA032431]

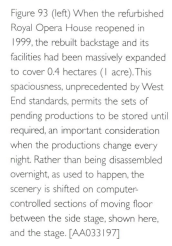

Figure 93 (left) When the refurbished Royal Opera House reopened in 1999, the rebuilt backstage and its facilities had been massively expanded to cover 0.4 hectares (1 acre). This spaciousness, unprecedented by West End standards, permits the sets of pending productions to be stored until required, an important consideration when the productions change every night. Rather than being disassembled overnight, as used to happen, the scenery is shifted on computer-controlled sections of moving floor between the side stage, shown here, and the stage. [AA033197]

Figure 94 A more substantial alternative to the thunder sheet was the thunder 'run', a wooden chute that zigzags down the stage wall, as surviving here at Her Majesty's Theatre. The noise created by a heavy ball rolling down the run gave the desired effect. Such relics evoke the 'blood and thunder' era of Edwardian theatre, when spectacle ruled. [AA020590]

Figure 95 (below) Different openings, or 'traps', were developed over time to get the performers on and off the stage in a range of exciting or dramatic ways. One of these was the star trap, which allows the actor to appear to erupt through the floor. This example, in the New London Theatre, was painted with feline stripes as part of the set for *Cats*. [AA032064]

Figure 96 The stage of the Dominion Theatre viewed from above. Though animated here by a blur of technicians, when devoid of sets and actors the stage seems a place in limbo. The limited space in the wings is typical of a West End theatre, though there is more space here than in many. [AA032019]

Figure 97 (above) Production lighting has become increasingly complex and now requires a bewildering array of spot- and floodlights, located above and to the sides of the stage as well as in the auditorium. To allow for checking, repairs or adjustment, the backstage lighting rigs in the Prince of Wales Theatre have here been lowered to the stage. [AA020847]

Figure 98 (below) The 'prompt corner', the illuminated area tucked away behind the proscenium, here occupies its traditional position on the actor's left-hand side of the stage in Her Majesty's Theatre. Its purpose is to enable the stage manager to oversee the performance and operate the safety curtain. The breaks in the stage floor reveal the 'bridges', sections that can be raised or lowered to suit the demands of the production. [AA020587]

Figure 99 (above) Short cinematic presentations were featuring in certain West End variety theatres by 1903. The projection boxes were usually installed in the auditorium below the circle, but this later example from the London Coliseum was positioned at the back of the stage. [AA025421]

Figure 100 Viewed here from the orchestra pit, the modest size of the stage at the Cambridge Theatre is even more evident when empty of scenery. Playhouses built between the First and Second World Wars were generally devised on a much smaller, more intimate scale than their Edwardian predecessors. [AA020425]

Figure 101 (below) A 'prop table' in the Gielgud Theatre, with its top divided into labelled sections, to ensure that its contents are easily found, and returned to the same place in a darkened rear of stage. The term 'prop', deriving from property, refers to those items used during a production that are neither wardrobe nor scenery. [AA025589]

Scenes and sets

Figure 102 (above) Chris Floyd, scene painter, is seen here at the Players' Theatre, surrounded by scenery. The canvas pieces attached to tall lightweight timber frames are known as 'flats'. [AA032114]

Figure 103 (left) Not all the West End theatres had the space to build or paint their own sets on site, but relied instead on workshops elsewhere in the capital. Delivery of the scenery was via special tall 'get in' doors. As so many stages were below street level, these doors often had to be provided with hoists, as here at the Duke of York's Theatre. [AA025779]

Figure 104 (left) The Drury Lane Theatre Royal is unusually well equipped with rear and side stage areas, as befits its status as the premier playhouse in the capital. Until 2003 its scene dock contained rolled backcloths, the huge sheets of painted canvas that form the back of a set, stored on an elderly timber wall rack. [AA020410]

Figure 105 (right) A detail of the Cochrane Theatre's colour-spattered paint frame and the wall behind. [AA032360]

Figure 106 (above) This heavy metal safety door, adorned with graffiti by visiting companies, separates the Bloomsbury Theatre's stage from the adjoining storage area, the scene dock. [AA032841]

Figure 107 (left) The Cochrane Theatre was built as a training theatre for students at the adjoining Central School of Arts and Crafts, so it was provided with a range of workshops for set, scene and props production. This empty frame for painting backcloths is one of the last still in operation in the West End. [AA032357]

Figure 108 The Drury Lane Theatre Royal has been one of only a few West End theatres to have dedicated space for painting backcloths. Here a scene painter holds up the sketch he is about to transfer to the large piece of canvas behind. This is attached to a movable frame for ease of access. Only the upper part of the canvas is visible, the rest is below the floor. [AA020403]

Understage

Figure 109 These Austrian-made hydraulic rams were installed at the Drury Lane Theatre Royal in 1896 to enable two bridges to be raised, lowered or tilted to create spectacular effects. A further pair of bridges, powered by electric motors, was added in 1898. [AA020390]

Figure 110 The heart of the technician's domain, an understage crew room in the Piccadilly Theatre. [AA025343]

Figure 111 (below) The timber understage at Wyndham's Theatre is more typical of the West End theatres than are the steel girders of the Drury Lane Theatre Royal (see Fig 109), even though they are roughly contemporary. Modern staging has little need for traps and bridges, so the space has been put to other uses as workshops. [AA025739]

Figure 113 (above) Stage turntables, or 'revolves', were developed in Continental and American theatres in the late 19th century to make possible faster scene changes, but they were never widespread in the West End. This early 20th-century revolve at the London Palladium was replaced by new staging machinery in 2002. [AA020460]

Figure 112 (above) The Palace Theatre was provided with an ambitious three-level understage designed by the engineer Walter Dando. But going so deep has had unintended consequences – a stream of ground water flows continuously across the floor, a problem that also affects several other West End theatres. A significant amount of Dando's understage survives, though long disused. [AA020799]

Figure 114 A system that enabled the easy movement of scenery between the backstage and an out-of-town store was one of the requirements of the 1997–9 reconstruction of the Royal Opera House. This bespoke temporary storage area is below the stage level. Metal pallets or containers holding components of the sets rest on a conveyor until required. [AA033210]

Figure 115 (above) A traditional West End understage has two levels – the mezzanine, shown here at the Gielgud Theatre, and a lower part known as the 'cellar'. It was on the upper level that the machinery, such as the counterweighted stage bridge in the foreground, would have been operated by hand-powered winches. Few backstage spaces are as immaculately kept as this. [AA025590]

Figure 116 (below) As backstage space in a West End theatre was always at a premium, circulation between the stage, understage and fly floors was often very tight. Compact spiral staircases, like this one at Wyndham's Theatre, have provided one solution. [AA025742]

Figure 117 (above) Hydraulic power was often employed backstage; this relic in the Lyric Theatre is a hand-powered standby pump that worked the heavy iron safety curtain if the main supply failed. There were also five hydraulic stage bridges in this theatre, replaced by a revolve in the early 20th century. [AA020532]

Figure 118 The lowest level of the understage at St Martin's Theatre retains early drums and shafts for operating the stage bridges. Above are the upright 'guides' that held pieces of scenery after they had been dropped through the narrow cuts or openings in the stage floor known as 'sloats'. A smaller drum, just below the inserted ceiling, may have been used to operate a trap. This is one of the most complete ensembles of such machinery still left in the West End. [AA032881]

Figure 119 (left) Many understages contain an accumulation of obsolescent equipment and technology, reflecting various phases of alteration or modification for a specific production or just changing fashions in staging. This rectifier converts the mains supply from an alternating current to a direct current, serving an electric motor powering a stage revolve at the Lyric Theatre. [AA020536]

Figure 120 The 'grid', the lattice structure at the top of the fly tower that rises above the stage, is a key component of any flying system. In many theatres the wood and hemp of the early grids have been superseded by steel and wire, as here at the Victoria Palace Theatre. The roof above has a central lantern, a safety feature designed to be opened from elsewhere in the theatre in the event of a fire, to draw smoke upwards and away from the rest of the building. [AA032477]

Figure 121 The grid and one of the substantial trusses that support it in the London Coliseum, viewed from a lofty vantage point, the higher of the two galleries on the side wall that serve the flying system. The presence of so much metal in the fly tower shows Frank Matcham's innovatory approach to theatre design, though wood was not completely banished from the grid's construction. [AA025426]

Above stage: flying systems

Figure 122 The need to allow scenery to be hoisted above proscenium openings led to the raising of stage roofs in the late 19th century and the creation of fly towers. Pieces of cloth, elements of the set or lights are hung from long metal bars that can be raised or lowered from the galleries on the side walls, known as 'fly floors'. All the bars here at the Strand Theatre are empty, permitting a clear view. [AA032996]

Figure 123 (facing page) A fly floor. Originally, the 'flying' of the sets or cloths on or off the stage was done with ropes, or 'hemp lines', hauled by hand and tied off on a beam or 'fly rail'. Some West End theatres have continued to fly completely by hand, as here at the New Ambassadors Theatre. [AA025976]

Figure 124 Drums and shafts for the heavy lifting work were often to be found on the grid as well as in the understage. The Comedy Theatre has one of the most impressive collections of historic machinery, but the long-term prospects for the retention of such 'archaeological' remnants are uncertain. [AA025393]

Figure 125 The grid and its understage equivalent, the cellar, are the most inaccessible parts of the backstage. Many grids are reached by fixed vertical ladders, as here at the Bloomsbury Theatre. [AA032827]

Figure 126 In the London Palladium this sequence of raised cloths or drops was suspended from the grid. [AA020480]

Figure 127 The steel-framed grid of the Cochrane Theatre, lit from beneath, illustrating its form. This unusual view shows the wires from the flying bars emerging from pulley blocks. [AA032354]

Figure 128 The transformation of the backstage at the Royal Opera House in 1997–9 involved the fly tower being raised to a height of 37 metres above the stage. There are more than a hundred flying bars suspended from the new grid, all operated by mobile computer controls. [AA033212]

Figure 129 A detail of the movable wooden 'head blocks' at the edge of the grid in Wyndham's Theatre. Through these pass the hemp lines *en route* from the suspended flying bars to the fly floor on the side wall, allowing the former to be raised or lowered. Three, as here, or four lines for each bar are the norm. [AA025745]

Figure 130 The late 19th-century introduction of counterweights took much of the hard labour out of flying scenery. The adjustable weights are attached to lines that run in tracks down the side wall. In some theatres, as here at the Drury Lane Theatre Royal, these tracks reach all the way down to the stage. From the 1890s onwards most, though not all, new West End theatres installed such systems as a matter of course. [AA020377]

Figure 131 (below) The Gielgud Theatre has both wooden cleats for tying off the ropes that hold the sets or cloths suspended aloft and a counterweighted flying system. Spare weights can be seen lined up along the gallery floor while those in use are carried in cradles just visible behind the ropes. The coloured markings on the ropes let the operator know that the scenery has reached its correct position. [AA025597]

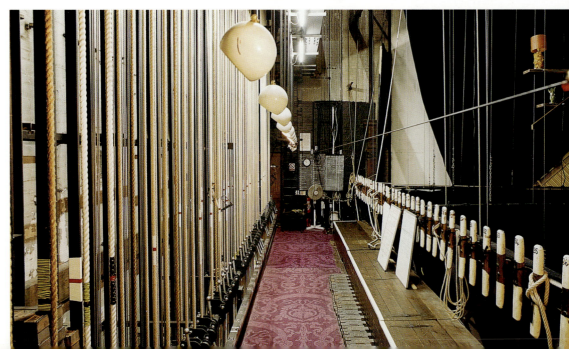

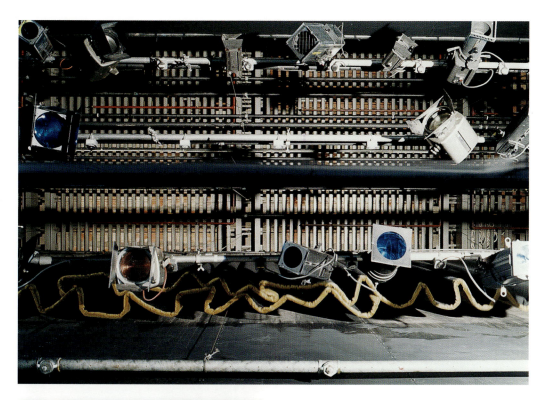

Figure 132 (above) A view looking up from the Cochrane Theatre's stage. This shows the metal safety curtain, with a drencher pipe intended to apply water to the curtain in the event of a fire, and the velvet edge of the house curtain. There are flying bars, mostly used for lights, and above is the metal grid from which they are suspended. [AA032349]

Figure 133 This notice in the Westminster Theatre relates to an aspect of the counterweighted flying system. The large number of theatres under construction or rebuilding in London from the late 19th century onwards encouraged the development of specialist firms, such as Frank Burkitt. Many of these businesses were located in South London, particularly in Lambeth and Southwark. [AA026023]

Figure 134 The rebuilding of its backstage in 1997–9 put the Royal Opera House at the forefront of international theatre design, not least in the replacement of a counterweighted flying system with computer-controlled motorised flying. The Nomad Motion Control Flying System may prove to be the precursor of things to come elsewhere in the West End. [AA033215]

Dressing rooms

Figure 135 As many of the West End theatres were built at a period when the status of the actor was low, their accommodation was often cramped, poorly lit and inconveniently located. This was certainly not the case with the principal actor's dressing rooms at the Albery Theatre, however, perhaps reflecting the influence of its first owner, the actor-manager Sir Charles Wyndham. [AA025695]

Figure 136 For the actor the dressing room is often a home from home for the duration of a particular role. This relatively spacious room in the Gielgud Theatre is for a lead actor or star. The light-edged mirror is the focus of a room that otherwise lacks any hint of glamour. [AA025606]

Figure 137 (below) Most theatres observe a clear hierarchy when it comes to dressing rooms. While the stars may have individual spaces the rest of the cast often has to share, as here in the room at the Apollo Victoria provided for members of the chorus of *Starlight Express*. [AA032294]

Figure 138 (above) The costumes for *Cats* in the New London Theatre. Such costumes have to be maintained and repaired during the production run but are rarely made on site. From the late 19th century onwards costume-making was increasingly contracted out to specialist suppliers. [AA032084]

Figure 139 (right) Tony Raban, a wigdresser, preparing for the next performance at the Prince Edward Theatre. [AA020690]

Costumes

Figure 140 The wigs for *Phantom of the Opera* at Her Majesty's Theatre, each an individual creation, fitted to a single actor, and made from human hair. [AA020611]

Figure 141 The roller skates from the long-running production of *Starlight Express* at the Apollo Victoria. The show closed in 2002. [AA032281]

Figure 142 (facing page) A list of costume problems for a production of *Little Women*, in rehearsal at the Bloomsbury Theatre. [AA032835]

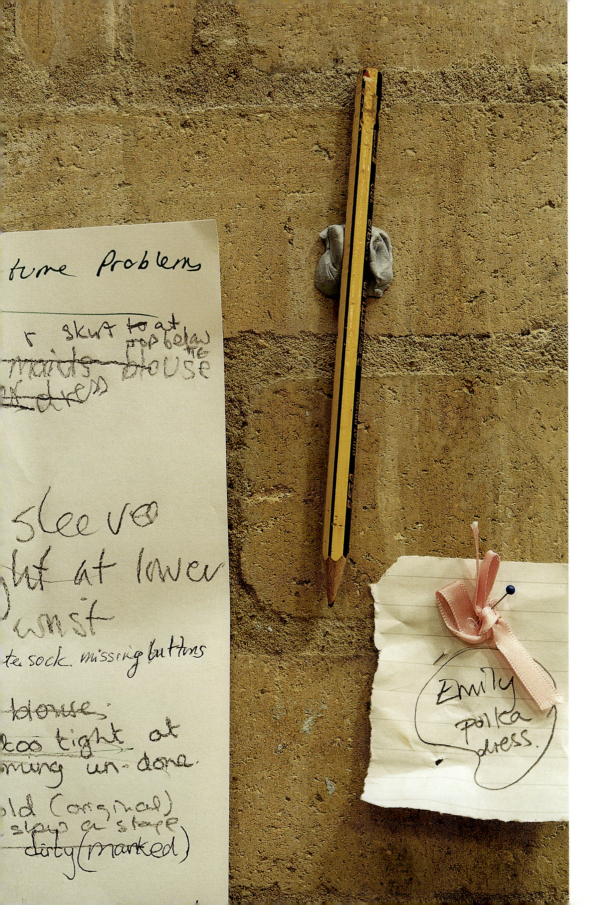

85

Stage door ••••

Figure 143 The Albery Theatre and Wyndham's Theatre both back on to the same court. Latterly they have shared a single stage door, with access to Wyndham's being via a bridge. The 'pairing' of theatres – back-to-back, side-by-side or at either end of a block – was a feature of the theatre-building boom around 1900. [AA025650]

Figure 144 Most stage doors are located at the side or to the rear of the theatres, but at the Garrick Theatre the door is in a separate block, on the left side of the photograph. This building houses the dressing rooms and is linked to the backstage below ground. [AA020244]

Figure 145 The Cerberus of the backstage entrance, the stage doorman, sits in his tiny room, as here at the Cambridge Theatre, overseeing comings and goings, taking deliveries and handing out messages and dressing-room keys to actors as they arrive for work. [AA020438]

Figure 146 (below) The stage doorman's work is often, though not invariably, solitary. This view is from the London Palladium. [AA020492]

Living with the Legacy

by Peter Longman,
Director of The Theatres Trust

One theatrical entrepreneur, Sir Cameron Mackintosh, has been quoted as describing them as 'the last Victorian relics that haven't been modernised', while another, Lord Andrew Lloyd-Webber, has apparently regretted the fact that he is not allowed to demolish them, so that they can be replaced with new ones. London's West End possibly has the greatest concentration of theatre buildings in the world open fifty-two weeks a year, and has more shows and attracts bigger audiences even than New York. But the buildings are old – only a handful have been created since the Second World War – and most of them still reflect the social and technical demands of theatregoing of a hundred years ago.

Nevertheless, audiences seem to like the plush and gilt, and the Victorian and Edwardian opulence, and the way in which the architects of that period managed to bring audiences and performers together. The West End's theatreland is one of Britain's biggest tourist attractions, earning more currency than the country's entire advertising, accountancy and consultancy sectors, and hugely more than its film and television industry. The trouble is that this money does not go back into theatre buildings. Owning a theatre building is not a good way of making money. For every hit show – and there are many that do not survive – it is the producers and the investors, not the theatre owners, who occasionally strike it rich. That is one reason why so few of our theatre buildings have been modernised. Those that have been built or modernised over the last twenty-five years have nearly all had outside help, either directly from the Government, like the National Theatre, or through the National Lottery. To put matters into perspective, the Lottery grant that enabled the Royal Court Theatre to be so splendidly modernised in 2000, was more than the combined profits made by all the playhouses on London's famous Shaftesbury Avenue since the Second World War. And even if a theatre owner in the commercial sector could afford to rebuild, the cost of doing so might well be as much as ten times the amount the theatre would then fetch if sold. But if the site was to be cleared, and planning permission obtained for a different, more commercial use, then its value would soar.

The Theatres Trust was set up by Act of Parliament in 1976 to protect theatres. The Government appoints the members of its governing body and gives it a small grant, now channelled through English Heritage. Theatres are the only non-ecclesiastical type of building to have their own statutory body set up to protect and improve them. In the 1970s, theatres all over the country were threatened by rising land values. With the demand for city-centre offices and retail outlets exceeding supply, and the possibility of being able to build high, theatres, with their comparatively large and often prominent sites, were a tempting prospect for developers. By the time the Trust was created, over 85 per cent of the 1,100 theatres that had stood in 1914 had been either completely destroyed or altered beyond recognition, and only about 5 per cent remained in use for their original intended purpose. Around thirty-five of the forty or so in the outer London boroughs had been lost. Even in London's West End half a dozen went, and a further fifteen, or nearly one-third of today's total stock, had been threatened at one time or another over the previous twenty years (Fig 147).

Although theatres are now recognised as a unique and wonderful set of buildings, they were not greatly revered by architectural historians of earlier times. They were seen as vulgar and commercial, the work of pragmatic populists, out to achieve maximum effect on a minimal budget, shoddily constructed and aiming to please a mass audience. They were perceived as lacking the intellectual rigour and seriousness of architecture with more high-minded aspirations. Even when many previously reviled Victorian buildings were re-evaluated, theatres were seen as less important to keep.

Today, less elitist attitudes prevail. These no longer exclude appreciation of theatre buildings, and the merits of Frank Matcham and his peers, those who built many of London's theatres, are recognised.

Figure 147 The auditorium of the former Carlton Theatre, converted to use as a cinema in 1979. [AA025464]

The work of The Theatres Trust extends throughout the United Kingdom, and while there are still many cases of theatre buildings being threatened with demolition for other more lucrative uses, in the West End this is now very rare. This is partly because most of the West End's theatres are now 'listed' by the Government for their architectural or historic interest. Of the fifty mainstream theatres in the West End, as defined for the survey presented here, three are listed at Grade I, ten at Grade II* and twenty-three at Grade II. Many are given further protection by being in conservation areas and by specific policies in the relevant local authority's development plans. For instance, much of the West End lies in the City of Westminster, whose development plans include a policy that planning permission will not be granted for a change of use from buildings used or previously used as theatres other than back to a theatre use.

Furthermore, the policy states that in those very exceptional circumstances where it is necessary to redevelop a theatre, a suitable replacement has to be provided within a stated period. And any planning application that affects a theatre building, whether or not it is still in use, has to be referred to The Theatres Trust for advice.

This does not mean, however, that The Theatres Trust and English Heritage have nothing to do in the West End. The buildings may be wonderful, but they were built for a different age and for different types of performances from modern ones. Many people do not realise that, a hundred years ago, theatres were designed to reflect a very class-conscious social structure. Only those in the best seats at the front of the stalls and in the dress circle could expect to come in through the front door, or to have adequate toilet and bar facilities. There was a barrier across the stalls, behind which most of the audience was crammed on to tightly packed benches, and where the sightlines were often obscured by pillars and the overhanging circle above them. Here, in the 'pit', were some of the cheapest seats in the theatre (see Fig 67). The top gallery, often affectionately known as 'the gods', was also generally comprised of benches and had minimal bar and toilet facilities. When C J Phipps was asked to design the present version of Her Majesty's Theatre on the Haymarket, his brief demanded that he provide for five different social classes, each with their own entrances, exits and facilities, and in such a way that as far as possible they should not meet or be aware of each other's existences. In some theatres that started their careers as music halls, it was not anticipated that respectable ladies would visit the bar at all, or therefore need to go to the toilet, so these facilities were simply not provided for them.

The result today, therefore, is that many theatres still have inadequate basic facilities, cramped entrance foyers that were never intended to serve the whole audience, and not enough toilets or bar space to meet modern standards. Many theatre seats are uncomfortably small for the better-nourished audiences of the 21st century. Longer legs have to squeeze into narrow rows and tiers. Whilst audiences may be prepared to compromise comfort to see a fringe production in a 'found space', they do not expect to have to do the same for top-price tickets in one of the world's most famous theatres. Current legislation to ensure that disabled people have adequate access to public buildings is admirable, but for old theatres, which operate on many different levels with complex arrangements of staircases, complying with the new Disability Discrimination Act (see p 95) is going to be especially difficult (Fig 148). Providing air-conditioning and proper ventilation is also a real challenge, not least because of the noise levels. No one wants to hear the whirl of an air-conditioning unit at a quiet and intense moment of the action.

Figure 148 A staircase at the Garrick Theatre. [AA020216]

Backstage in the West End is generally far from glamorous. Here there is less likely to be any decorative detail to damage, but that does not mean that these parts of the building are without historic interest. Actors may be happy to put up with some discomfort, knowing that they are playing where famous stars have preceded them, but there is a limit as to what they can be expected to suffer, especially on a long run. Even so-called 'star' dressing rooms often have little or no natural light and ventilation, and toilet and shower facilities are often sparse and inconveniently located.

Stage machinery and equipment can also be a problem. The photographs in this book include many romantic and atmospheric views of installations that are now museum pieces in their own right. Using hemp lines to raise and lower scenery means hard work for the stage crew and it is likely that future health and safety legislation will make fully mechanised

Figure 149 Mirror panels on stage at the Garrick Theatre, reflecting the auditorium. [AA020231]

'flying' compulsory. The surface of a Victorian stage was usually raked, sloping up from the front to the back to improve sightlines. Now scenery is generally made to fit over a flat stage, so the actual boards are unlikely to be those trodden by famous actors of past generations (Fig 149). But if you flatten the stage it is very easy to ruin the carefully judged sightlines that enabled those actors furthest away from the audience to be seen and to 'upstage' those nearer the front. The traditional wooden Victorian stage, with its range of traps and bridges for scene changes and sudden appearances and disappearances, was a highly successful and adaptable machine, but very labour intensive. Innovations such as the large revolve in the middle of the stage at the London Palladium were

costly to install, and were a major part of the fabric. Though it was well known to television audiences throughout Britain from its use in the finale to the famous television show *Sunday Night at the London Palladium*, the revolve clearly could not have coped with the flying car in *Chitty Chitty Bang Bang!* With the agreement of English Heritage and specialist advice from The Theatres Trust and members of the Association of British Theatre Technicians, it has been photographed, recorded and removed. Most directors and designers today would rather have a modular stage floor that they can adapt according to the needs of the specific production.

In theatres, building maintenance has often suffered at the expense of production costs – after all, money spent on a set or securing a star actor can be seen to have an immediate impact and may generate quick returns by way of increased seat sales. Theatres in the West End generally concentrate on receiving shows rather than producing them. They are in effect spaces available for hire, and in the past were often owned by companies who ultimately had no direct interest in the theatre business. Indeed, several theatres were acquired simply in anticipation of the day when consent would be agreed for them to be demolished and replaced by something more lucrative. As most of the West End's theatres have come to be acquired by people who are in the theatre business, it has been possible to employ building specialists to undertake proper forward planning, including regular inspections identifying the urgency of projected future works. Keeping a building log, drawing together documentary research and doing a proper analysis of the historic fabric and the building's history can help to generate informed decisions, particularly when consent is to be sought to make major alterations that may affect the historic nature or interest of the building concerned.

In day-to-day terms, the need to maintain a theatre licence will be uppermost in the mind of management. Local authority licensing teams inspect theatres annually to ensure that the premises are safe for audiences, staff and performers. They may also investigate complaints from local residents and have the power to close a production that is overly noisy. In an ideal world, theatre managements would find permanent solutions to problems such as disabled access and poor toilets and circulation, but current limited budgets mean that these are tackled only temporarily and in an ad hoc way. It is not just the budgets that are restricting, though. Timescales often are too, for it is always hard to predict when a theatre will be 'dark'. As each new production opens, it is impossible to say how long a run it will achieve. And if you are running a theatre on a commercial basis, a theatre closed, for whatever reason, is a theatre that is not producing any income.

So what does the future hold? A theatre needs the ritual of performances in order to be appreciated. The atmosphere of arriving with a crowd, taking your seats together and waiting for the lights to go down and the curtain up, is an essential part of the process. The survival of these amazing buildings is dependent on people continuing to want to buy tickets for plays and shows. Good new writing and productions are required if the present pattern of theatregoing is to endure into the future. That would ensure that the buildings will still be needed.

But we cannot expect audiences to continue indefinitely to visit theatre buildings that were put up more than a century ago. Making them more comfortable and more accessible is crucial to their survival – and that means a financial investment. Whilst many of our museums and art galleries and subsidised theatres have had National Lottery funding, most of the West End's theatres are commercially or privately owned and have therefore not been considered a priority for either Arts Council or Heritage Lottery Fund grants. The high costs of land and buildings in the West End mean that putting up new theatres is simply not an option. That is why The Theatres Trust has been working with the Society of London Theatre and leading theatre owners to assess what needs to be done to find ways of securing the necessary money. Funding aside, all our findings to date suggest that it is possible to modernise these buildings without jeopardising their special historic interest or character. This photographic survey records a splendid and often unseen part of Britain's theatrical heritage, at a crucial moment in its long history. The British tourist industry and London's reputation as the theatrical centre of the world greatly depend upon these buildings and their continued existence.

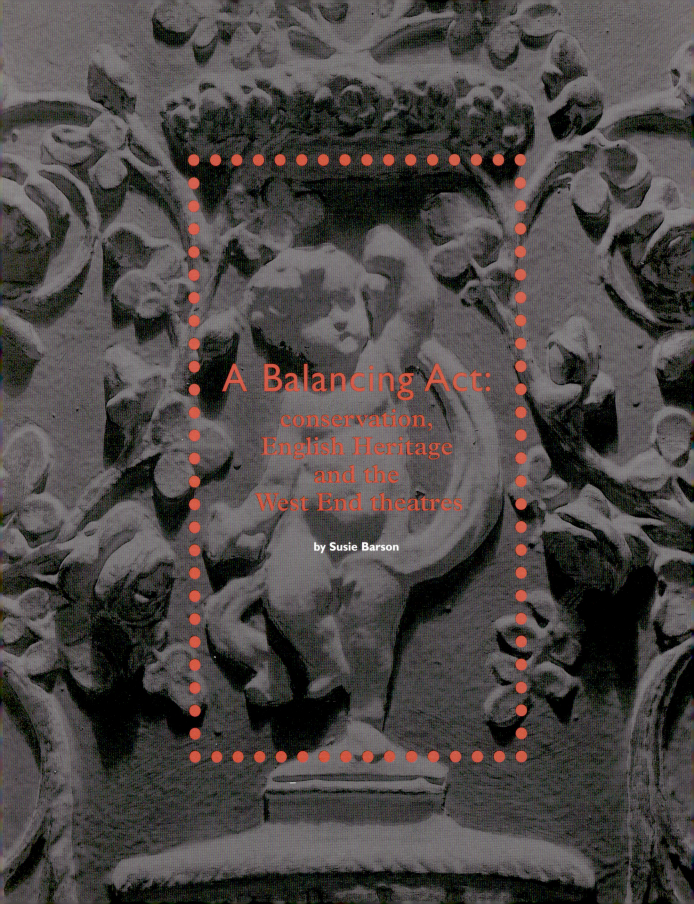

A Balancing Act:
conservation, English Heritage and the West End theatres

by Susie Barson

English Heritage has a range of responsibilities relating to the historic environment. It strives to encourage the appreciation and understanding of historic buildings, through survey and publication, as here, as well as through opening properties to the public. The organisation has a parallel and no-less-important duty to ensure that historic buildings are not subjected to inappropriate interventions that compromise their significance, in short that the principles of building conservation are properly observed.

That thirty-six West End theatres are 'listed' buildings has important implications. Inclusion on the statutory 'list' of buildings of architectural or historic interest is a formal recognition of significance, and accordingly carries with it a measure of control over what can be done to the building. Once a building is 'listed', formal permission from the local planning authority, known as 'listed building consent' (LBC), must by law be applied for and obtained for any works of alteration or extension that would affect its architectural or historic character. In London, local planning authorities refer all LBC applications affecting theatres to English Heritage for comment. These applications are similarly referred to The Theatres Trust, and to national amenity societies concerned with the historic environment, the Georgian Group, the Victorian Society and the 20th Century Society being of relevance in this context. Once an application has been considered, the local planning authority may grant consent, with English Heritage approval, or refuse to grant LBC irrespective of the view of English Heritage. Outright refusal is rare, and most applications are approved or revised to the satisfaction of all interested parties. A more detailed explanation of the operation of the planning system as it affects the historic environment is set out in current government planning policy guidance.

English Heritage shares with London's planning authorities and other interested parties responsibility for safeguarding the West End's 'listed' theatres, the gems that are illustrated here. Since the 1990s there has been considerable pressure from the theatre owners to permit significant change. English Heritage recognises that most West End theatres are commercial enterprises, subject to pressures for improvement and modernisation to attract new patrons. Live performance is one of the chief reasons that people from all over the world visit London. They come to see Shakespeare, or modern experimental theatre, or elaborate 'block-busting' musicals. They also come to enjoy the ambience of the theatres – the architectural surroundings. But, above all, they come to have a good evening out. Modern expectations of comfort and accessibility are high. Theatre owners and producers are keen to meet these requirements, as well as to maximise profits to recoup the costs of mounting lavish productions.

One of the chief factors driving pressure for change in the West End theatres is the desire of management groups to unify and enlarge front-of-house access and facilities, breaking down the original hierarchies of separate entrances, circulation areas and bars. Other aspirations are the enhancement of sightlines by altering seating arrangements, and of comfort by improving ventilation and air-conditioning. Sometimes such improvements can be managed without undue detriment to the character of the interior. More immediately damaging to the architectural integrity of the auditorium has been the outward spread of fittings specific to productions, such as extra stages, and more permanent structures for lighting, sound rigs and the like. Delicate plasterwork on balcony fronts can easily be obscured or damaged by the insensitive siting of lighting bars (Fig 150). Other conservation issues affecting 'listed' theatres include tendencies to erect new exterior signage, and brighter lighting in the circulation spaces.

A new challenge facing theatre owners, and one that will have a significant impact on the buildings, is the implementation of Part 3 of the Disability Discrimination Act (1995), which is due to come into effect in 2004. Through this legislation managers of public buildings are obliged to address all levels of disability, and to make reasonable adjustments to

provide physical access to all areas, some hitherto out of the reach of some patrons. Other challenges arise from regulations concerning asbestos, whereby every theatre has to be surveyed for and cleared of this material, and new fire regulations, which require the installation of extensive fire-alarm systems. These regulatory calls on money often mean that there is less to spend on the basic maintenance of the fabric of the building.

Maintenance and non-urgent repair are unavoidable duties for all building owners. In the West End theatres this responsibility lies with the lessees and the managements. In theatres the problems of maintenance and repair can be particularly onerous, ranging from leaking roofs, to failing stone and terracotta, and flooding in basements caused by central London's rising water table. The servicing of ageing heating, cooling and ventilation systems also takes time and money. Unfortunately, commercial realities mean that investors have the first call on profits from a show before building-related matters can be addressed.

English Heritage has considerable experience of dealing with proposals for alterations in theatres, and is well placed to offer advice on the best way forward. Advice can also be obtained from The Theatres Trust and from local planning authority officers. This applies whatever part of a building proposals might affect. Statutory 'listing' covers the whole building – in theatres, the backstage areas are every bit as 'listed' as are the auditoria. To meet the need for advice English Heritage produced a leaflet about theatre conservation in 1995, which set out some general guidelines on the control of alterations (*Theatres: A Guide to Theatre Conservation from English Heritage*). On the issue of original or historic stage machinery, which may either be redundant or no longer conform to health and safety regulations, this guide recommended that, where possible, it be left

Figure 150 (facing page) Lighting bars across balcony fronts at the Garrick Theatre. [AA020204]

in situ and new equipment installed around it. This approach has been successful, as at Her Majesty's Theatre, where hydraulic lifts, computer-controlled sets and smoke effects for the long-running production of the *Phantom of the Opera* were installed alongside machinery of the 1890s.

English Heritage considers each case on its own merits, and, where warranted, with a sympathetic eye. Historical research and recording may often be necessary to underpin the informed consideration and any subsequent acceptance of schemes of alteration. The expectation normally is that changes that will affect architectural and historic character should be kept to a minimum, with new work avoiding important features where possible. The basic principle that is observed concerning theatre interiors and their decoration is that those elements which are original, historic or part of the theatre's special interest should remain intact, and that if any parts of such work are to be removed, or new work added, interventions should be of a high quality, sensitively designed so as to be in keeping with, or a complement to, the existing architecture. If a theatre has already been extensively altered there is likely to be more scope for change, as was the case with the alterations in 2000 to the Royal Court Theatre in Sloane Square.

English Heritage is well aware that most theatres are commercial enterprises, and endeavours to balance changing standards of comfort and safety with the preservation of the special architectural or historic interest of buildings. Justifications put forward in support of proposed changes to listed theatres are fully and carefully considered. In a collaborative process, the desire for alteration can be weighed against the capabilities and limitations of the historic buildings. Theatres have always been subject to change. English Heritage understands this when advising on adaptation of the buildings to ensure their continued use for the future, while also insisting on the importance of conservation, not least as a means to the same end. Sir Cameron Mackintosh's significant investment in his theatres, the latest phase of which was announced in June 2003, is a major next step, warmly welcomed by English Heritage in a close working relationship.

London is home to the majority of Britain's theatrical institutions, and, in the last twenty years, has become a leader in the production of musicals for performance throughout the world. Theatres for opera, ballet, musicals and plays help make London a world-class cultural centre, with a unique concentration in the West End. Diversification is currently seen as necessary in order to keep audiences coming. Changes in this direction have been seen in the last few years in the employment of national and international film, television and pop celebrities on the London stage. In all this the value of the buildings themselves must not be overlooked. Wider problems related to transport, public safety and cleanliness in the streets are being – and need further to be – addressed if the West End theatres, jewels in London's crown, are to continue to shine.

West End Theatres: a gazetteer

This gazetteer is largely derived from John Earl and Michael Sell (eds), *The Theatres Trust Guide to British Theatres 1750–1950: A Gazetteer*.

Adelphi Theatre
Strand, WC2
1930, Ernest Schaufelberg, architect, incorporating parts of Victorian successors to the Sans Pareil of 1806; restored 1993, Jaques Muir and Partners, architects
(Listed Grade II; NMR File 106816; Fig 5)

Albery Theatre
St Martin's Lane, WC2
1903 as New Theatre, W G R Sprague, architect, for Sir Charles Wyndham
(Listed Grade II; NMR File 106817; Figs 3, 69, 135 & 143)

Aldwych Theatre
Aldwych, WC2
1905, W G R Sprague, architect
(Listed Grade II; NMR File 106818; Figs 37, 40, 47 & 74)

Apollo Theatre
Shaftesbury Avenue, W1
1901, Lewen Sharp, architect, with Hubert van Hooydonk
(Listed Grade II; NMR File 106820)

Apollo Victoria Theatre
Wilton Road, SW1
1930 as New Victoria Cinema, E Wamsley Lewis and W E Trent, architects
(Listed Grade II*; NMR File 106821; Figs 64, 137 & 141)

Arts Theatre
Great Newport Street, WC2
1927, Arts Theatre Club basement theatre, P Morley Horder, architect; reconstructed 1951 and remodelled 2001
(Not listed; NMR File 106822; Figs 22 & 89)

Bloomsbury Theatre
Gordon Street, WC1
1964–9 as the Collegiate Theatre for University College London, Fello Atkinson of James Cubitt & Partners, architects
(Not listed; NMR File 106823; Figs 6, 49, 106, 125 & 142)

Cambridge Theatre
Earlham Street, WC2
1930, Wimperis, Simpson and Guthrie, with Serge Chermayeff, architects; restored 1988, Carl Toms, architect
(Listed Grade II; NMR File 106824; Figs 79, 100 & 145)

Carlton Theatre (Odeon Cinema)
Haymarket, SW1
1927–8, Verity and Beverley, architects; converted 1979
(Not listed; NMR File 106825; Fig 147)

Cochrane Theatre
Southampton Row, WC1
1957–65 as the Jeanetta Cochrane training theatre for the Central School of Arts and Crafts, London County Council Architects' Department (R S Skilling); front of house remodelled 1992
(Not listed; NMR File 106826; Figs 73, 105, 107, 127 & 132)

Comedy Theatre
Panton Street, SW1
1881–4, Thomas Verity, architect; various 20th-century alterations
(Listed Grade II; NMR File 106827; Figs 35, 63, 65 & 124)

Criterion Theatre
Piccadilly Circus, W1
1873–4, Thomas Verity, architect; extended 1878 and altered 1883–4 by Verity; restored and altered 1992, RHWL, architects
(Listed Grade II*; NMR File 106828; Figs 27 & 78)

Dominion Theatre

Tottenham Court Road, WC1

1928–9 for Moss Empires, W and T R Milburn (William Milburn junior), architects; used mainly as a cinema from 1930 to the 1970s; variously altered

(Listed Grade II; NMR File 106829; Figs 72 & 96)

Donmar Warehouse

Earlham Street, WC2

1977 as The Warehouse, conversion for the Royal Shakespeare Company of a Victorian brewery vat room that had been made a rehearsal room in 1960 by Sir Donald Albery; reconstructed 1992

(Not listed; NMR File 106830; Fig 62)

Drury Lane Theatre Royal

(often known as Theatre Royal Drury Lane)

Catherine Street, WC2

1811–12 as the fourth theatre on the site since 1663, Benjamin Dean Wyatt, architect; auditorium rebuilt 1921–2 by Emblin Walker, Jones and Cromie, architects

(Listed Grade I; NMR File 106831; Figs 9, 31, 33, 86, 90, 104, 108, 109 & 130)

Duchess Theatre

Catherine Street, WC2

1929, Ewen S Barr, architect, with Marc-Henri Levy and Gaston Laverdet

(Not listed; NMR File 106832; Figs 12 & 60)

Duke of York's Theatre

St Martin's Lane, WC2

1892 as Trafalgar Square Theatre, Walter Emden, architect; altered and restored 1979, RHWL, architects

(Listed Grade II; NMR File 106833; Fig 103)

Fortune Theatre

Russell Street, WC2

1924, Ernest Schaufelberg, architect

(Listed Grade II; NMR File 106834; Fig 21)

Garrick Theatre

Charing Cross Road, WC2

1889, Walter Emden, with C J Phipps, architects

(Listed Grade II*; NMR File 106835; Figs 39, 48, 144, 148, 149 & 150)

Gielgud Theatre

Shaftesbury Avenue, W1

1906 as Hicks Theatre, W G R Sprague, architect; known from 1909 to 1994 as the Globe Theatre

(Listed Grade II; NMR File 106836; Figs 20, 101, 115, 131 & 136)

Haymarket Theatre Royal

(often known as Theatre Royal, Haymarket)

Haymarket, SW1

1821, John Nash, architect; replacing a theatre of 1720; auditorium rebuilt 1879–80, C J Phipps, architect, and again 1905, C Stanley Peach with S D Adshead, architects

(Listed Grade I; NMR File 94937; Figs 25, 51, 59, 70 & 80)

Her Majesty's Theatre

Haymarket, SW1

1897 as the third theatre on the site since 1705, C J Phipps, architect, with Romaine Walker, for Herbert Beerbohm Tree

(Listed Grade II*; NMR File 106837; Figs 17, 45, 94, 98 & 140)

London Coliseum

(often known as the Coliseum)

St Martin's Lane, WC2

1904 as a variety theatre, Frank Matcham, architect, for Oswald Stoll; used as an opera house since 1968

(Listed Grade II*; NMR File 95899; Figs 42, 75, 99 & 121)

London Palladium

(often known as the Palladium)

Argyll Street, W1

1910 as a variety theatre, Frank Matcham, architect, retaining the façade of the Corinthian Bazaar of 1868, Owen Lewis, architect

(Listed Grade II*; NMR File 106839; Figs 13, 19, 85, 113, 126 & 146)

Lyceum Theatre

Wellington Street, WC2

1904, Bertie Crewe, architect, retaining the façade of 1834, Samuel Beazley, architect; used as a ballroom from 1945; reconverted and stagehouse rebuilt 1996, Holohan Architects

(Listed Grade II*; NMR File 106839; Fig 4)

Lyric Theatre

Shaftesbury Avenue, W1

1888, C J Phipps, architect; altered and restored

(Listed Grade II; NMR File 106840; Figs 117 & 119)

New Ambassadors Theatre

(often known as Ambassadors Theatre)

West Street, WC2

1913, W G R Sprague, architect

(Listed Grade II; NMR File 106819; Figs 7, 32 & 123)

New London Theatre

Drury Lane, WC2

1971–3, Michael Percival & Associates, architects, with Paul Tvrtovic; replacing the New Middlesex Theatre of Varieties of 1911

(Not listed; NMR File 106841; Figs 10, 23, 82, 95 & 138)

Palace Theatre

Cambridge Circus, W1

1891 as the Royal English Opera House, T E Collcutt, G H Holloway and J G Buckle, architects, for Richard D'Oyly Carte; converted to variety theatre 1892, Walter Emden, architect

(Listed Grade II*; NMR File 106843; Figs 26, 53, 67, 81 & 112)

Peacock Theatre

Portugal Street, WC2

1960 as the Royalty Theatre, Lewis Solomon and Kaye and Partners, architects, replacing the London Opera House of 1910–11

(Not listed; NMR File 106844; Figs 38, 87 & 92)

Phoenix Theatre

Charing Cross Road, WC2

1930, Sir Giles Gilbert Scott, Bertie Crewe and Cecil Masey, architects, with Theodore Komisarjevsky

(Listed Grade II; NMR File 106845; Fig 30)

Piccadilly Theatre

Denman Street, W1

1928, Bertie Crewe with Edward Albert Stone, architects; interior redesigned 1955

(Not listed; NMR File 106846; Figs 76 & 110)

Players' Theatre

The Arches, Villiers Street, WC2

1946, a neo-Victorian music hall in railway arches, reviving one that first opened here in 1866–7 as The Arches; a cinema from 1910 to 1946. Closed 2002

(Not listed; NMR File 106847; Figs 55 & 102)

Playhouse Theatre

Northumberland Avenue, WC2

1882 as the Royal Avenue Theatre, F H Fowler and Hill, architects; interior rebuilt 1907, Detmar Blow and Fernand Billerey, architects; restored 1987, Graham Berry, architect

(Listed Grade II; NMR File 106848; Figs 54 & 56)

Prince Edward Theatre

Old Compton Street, W1

1929–30, Edward Albert Stone, architect, with Marc-Henri Levy and Gaston Laverdet; variously altered for use as a dinner/dance hall and cinema; restored 1978 and 1992–3, RHWL, architects

(Not listed; NMR File 106849; Figs 66, 88 & 139)

Prince of Wales Theatre

Coventry Street, W1

1937, Robert Cromie, architect, replacing the Prince's Theatre of 1884; interior altered 1963

(Listed Grade II; NMR File 106850; Figs 36 & 97)

Queen's Theatre

Shaftesbury Avenue, W1

1907–8, W G R Sprague, architect; front of house rebuilt and auditorium restored 1958–9, Bryan Westwood and Hugh Casson, architects

(Listed Grade II; NMR File 106851)

Royal Opera House

Bow Street, Covent Garden, WC2

1857–8 as the third theatre on the site since 1732, Edward M Barry, architect; variously altered and extended; new stagehouse and restoration 1997–9, Dixon Jones BDP, architects

(Listed Grade I; NMR File 81690; Figs 9, 44, 93, 114, 128 & 134)

St Martin's Theatre

West Street, WC2

1916, W G R Sprague, architect

(Listed Grade II; NMR File 106853; Figs 29, 58 & 118)

Saville Theatre (UGC Cinema)

Shaftesbury Avenue, W1

1931, T P Bennett and Son, architects; converted to cinema use 1970, William Ryder and Associates, architects

(Listed Grade II; NMR File 106854)

Savoy Theatre

Savoy Court, Strand, WC2

1881, C J Phipps, architect; interior rebuilt 1929, Frank A Tugwell, architect, with Basil Ionides; entrance 1929, Easton and Robertson, architects; restored 1993, Whitfield Partners, architects

(Listed Grade II*; NMR File 87235; Figs 11, 24, 41 & 71)

Shaftesbury Theatre

Shaftesbury Avenue, WC2

1911 as New Prince's Theatre, Bertie Crewe, architect

(Listed Grade II; NMR File 106855; Fig 77)

Soho Theatre

Dean Street, W1

1999–2000, Paxton Locher Architects in a conversion of the former West End Synagogue in a building of 1964

(Not listed; NMR File 106856; Figs 43 & 50)

Strand Theatre

Aldwych, WC2

1905 as the Waldorf Theatre, W G R Sprague, architect, with Hubert van Hooydonk

(Listed Grade II; NMR File 106857; Figs 34, 57, 61 & 122)

Vaudeville Theatre

Strand, WC2

1870, C J Phipps, architect; front rebuilt 1891 by Phipps; the remainder largely rebuilt 1926, Robert Atkinson, architect

(Listed Grade II; NMR File 106858; Fig 91)

Victoria Palace Theatre

Victoria Street, SW1

1911 as a variety theatre, Frank Matcham, architect

(Listed Grade II; NMR File 106859; Figs 15, 28 & 120)

Westminster Theatre

Palace Street, SW1

1923–4 conversion of a chapel of 1766 for a cinema, J Stanley Beard, architect; converted to be a theatre, 1931; remodelled 1965–6, John and Sylvia Reid, architects; closed 2002

(Not listed; NMR File 106860; Figs 8, 18 & 133)

Whitehall Theatre

Whitehall, SW1

1930, Edward Albert Stone, architect, with Marc-Henri Levy and Gaston Laverdet; restored 1985

(Listed Grade II; NMR File 106861; Figs 16, 46, 68 & 84)

Windmill Theatre

Great Windmill Street, W1

c 1909 as a cinema; converted 1931, F Edward Jones, architect; variously reconverted since 1964, latterly as a pole-dancing club

(Not listed; NMR File 106852)

Wyndham's Theatre

Charing Cross Road, WC2

1899, W G R Sprague, architect, for Charles Wyndham

(Listed Grade II*; NMR File 106880; Figs 14, 52, 83, 111, 116, 129 & 143)

Further Reading

Andrews, Richard 2002. *The London Theatre Guide*. London: Metro Publications

Booth, Michael R 1981. *Victorian Spectacular Theatre 1850–1910*. London: Routledge

Booth, Michael R and Kaplan, Joel H (eds) 1996. *The Edwardian Theatre*. Cambridge: Cambridge University Press

Buckle, James George 1888. *Theatre Construction and Maintenance*. London: The Stage Office

Buckle, James George and Woodrow, Ernest A E 1884. 'Theatre planning and construction'. *Building and Engineering News*, nos 1–28

Davies, Andrew 1987. *Other Theatres: The development of alternative and experimental theatre in Britain*. Basingstoke and London: Macmillan Education

Davis, Tracey C 2000. *The Economics of the British Stage 1800–1914*. Cambridge: Cambridge University Press

Earl, John and Sell, Michael (eds) 2000. *The Theatres Trust Guide to British Theatres 1750–1950: A gazetteer*. London: A & C Black

English Heritage 1995. *Theatres: A guide to theatre conservation from English Heritage*. London: English Heritage

Foulkes, R (ed) 1992. *British Theatre in the 1890s*. Cambridge: Cambridge University Press

Glasstone, Victor 1975. *Victorian and Edwardian Theatres*. London: Thames and Hudson

Howard, Diana 1970. *London Theatres and Music Halls 1850–1950*. London: The Library Association

Kilburn, Mike and Arzoz, Alberto 2002. *London's Theatres*. London: New Holland

Leacroft, Richard 1973. *The Development of the English Playhouse*. London: Eyre Methuen

Leacroft, Richard and Leacroft, Helen 1984. *Theatre and Playhouse: An illustrated survey of theatre buildings from ancient Greece to the present day*. London and New York: Methuen

Mackintosh, Iain and Sell, Michael (eds) 1982. *Curtains!!! or A New Life for Old Theatres*. London: Offord in association with the Curtains!!! Committee

Mander, Raymond and Mitchenson, Joe 1975. *Theatres of London*. London: New English Library

Maguire, Hugh 2000. 'The Victorian theatre as a home from home'. *Journal of Design History* 13/2

Pick, John 1983. *The West End: Mismanagement and snobbery*. Eastbourne: Offord

Reid, Francis 1995. *The ABC of Stage Technology*. London: A & C Black

Sachs, Edwin O 1896–7. 'Modern theatre stages'. *Engineering*, nos 1–30, 61–2

Sachs, Edwin O and Woodrow, Ernest A E 1896–8. *Modern Opera Houses and Theatres*, 3 vols. London: B T Batsford

Southern, Richard 1970. *The Victorian Theatres: A pictorial survey*. Newton Abbot: David & Charles

Survey of London 1960. *Vols XXIX and XXX: The Parish of St James Westminster, Part One. South of Piccadilly*. London: Athlone

Survey of London 1963. *Vols XXXI and XXXII: The Parish of St James Westminster, Part Two. North of Piccadilly*. London: Athlone

Survey of London 1966. *Vols XXXIII and XXXIV: The Parish of St Anne, Soho*. London: Athlone

Survey of London 1970. *Vol XXXV: The Theatre Royal, Drury Lane and the Royal Opera House, Covent Garden*. London: Athlone

Survey of London 1970. *Vol XXXVI: The Parish of St Paul, Covent Garden*. London: Athlone

Walker, Brian Mercer (ed) 1980. *Frank Matcham: Theatre architect*. Belfast: Blackstaff

Woodrow, Ernest A E 1892–4. 'Theatres'. *Building News*, nos 1–47

Information Sources

The Association of British Theatre Technicians
47 Bermondsey Street
London SE1 3XT
020 7403 3778
www.abtt.org.uk

Camden Local Studies and Archives Centre
Holborn Library
32–38 Theobalds Road
London WC1X 8PA
020 7974 6342
www.camden.gov.uk/localstudies

English Heritage
23 Savile Row
London W1S 2ET
020 7973 3000
www.english-heritage.org.uk

London Metropolitan Archives
40 Northampton Road
London EC1R 0HB
020 7332 3820
www.cityoflondon.gov.uk/lma

Mander and Mitchenson Theatre Collection
Jerwood Library of the Performing Arts
Trinity College of Music
King Charles Court
Old Royal Naval College
London SE10 9JF
020 8305 4426
email: rmangan@tcm.ac.uk

National Monuments Record (English Heritage)
Great Western Village
Kemble Drive
Swindon SN2 2GZ
01793 414600
www.english-heritage.org.uk/nmr

The Royal Institute of British Architects
66 Portland Place
London W1B 1AD
020 7580 5533
www.riba.org

Society of London Theatre
32 Rose Street
London WC2E 9ET
020 7557 6700
www.officiallondontheatre.co.uk

The Theatre Museum
1e Tavistock Street
London WC2E 7PR
020 7943 4700
www.theatremuseum.org

The Theatres Trust
22 Charing Cross Road
London WC2H 0QL
020 7836 8591
www.theatrestrust.org.uk

Westminster Archives Centre
10 St Ann's Street
London SW1P 2DE
020 7641 5180
www.westminster.gov.uk/archives

Westminster Reference Library
35 St Martin's Street
London WC2H 7HP
020 7641 4636
www.westminster.gov.uk/libraries

ENGLISH HERITAGE

NATIONAL
MONUMENTS
RECORD

For more information, why not use the National Monuments Record (NMR), the public archive of English Heritage.

The NMR contains comprehensive information on the archaeology and architecture of England, including air photographs and maritime sites. All the research and photography created while working on this project will be available there, along with historic photographs and a vast range of other material.

To find out more, call 01793 414600, write to NMR Enquiry and Research Services, National Monuments Record Centre, Great Western Village, Kemble Drive, Swindon SN2 2GZ, or visit our website: www.english-heritage.org.uk.

The *Theatres* Trust*

The Theatres Trust works to protect theatres and make them better, and assisted English Heritage with this publication. To find out more, call 020 7836 8591 or visit our website at www.theatrestrust.org.uk.

London's West End has a rich and unique collection of theatres, ranging in date from the early 19th century to the end of the 20th; more than fifty are located within an area of two square miles.

This book celebrates the working buildings at the heart of the British theatrical industry. It explores what constitutes a West End theatre, both culturally and physically, and outlines a brief history of the architecture, while also touching on the role of English Heritage and The Theatres Trust in theatre conservation. The striking photographs lead the reader on a wide-ranging tour starting at the entrance and exiting by the stage door, and taking in the front-of-house areas, the auditoria and the backstage spaces of some of London's most famous theatres. From the London Palladium to the Savoy Theatre, it offers glimpses of those areas not normally seen by the public, such as rehearsal spaces, dressing rooms and backstage areas. In doing so, this book enters the private realms of the theatre technicians and actors, and brings to light the theatre's hidden world.

The
Theatres
Trust *

ENGLISH HERITAGE

£14.99

ISBN 1-873592-74-4

9 781873 592748

T2-ECF-062